MW00533388

This book is dedicated to my friend Louise—
the only person I know who loves rocks, minerals,
and jewelry as much as I do!

About the Author

Ember Grant (Missouri) has been practicing the Craft for more than ten years. She has been contributing to *Llewellyn's Magical Almanac, Llewellyn's Herbal Almanac, Llewellyn's Spell-A-Day Almanac,* and *Llewellyn's Witches' Calendar* since 2003. Her writing has also appeared in *PanGaia, newWitch,* and *Circle* magazine.

To Write to the Author

If you wish to contact the author or would like more information about this book, please write to the author in care of Llewellyn Worldwide, and we will forward your request. Both the author and the publisher appreciate hearing from you and learning of your enjoyment of this book and how it has helped you. Llewellyn Worldwide cannot guarantee that every letter written to the author can be answered, but all will be forwarded. Please write to:

Ember Grant
℅ Llewellyn Worldwide
2143 Wooddale Drive
Woodbury, MN 55125-2989

Please enclose a self-addressed stamped envelope for reply,
or $1.00 to cover costs. If outside the USA, enclose
an international postal reply coupon.

Many of Llewellyn's authors have websites with additional information and resources. For more information, please visit our website at: www.llewellyn.com.

THE
– BOOK OF –
CRYSTAL SPELLS

MAGICAL USES FOR STONES, CRYSTALS, MINERALS ... AND EVEN SAND

EMBER GRANT

Llewellyn Publications
Woodbury, Minnesota

The Book of Crystal Spells: Magical Uses for Stones, Crystals, Minerals… and Even Sand © 2013 by Ember Grant. All rights reserved. No part of this book may be used or reproduced in any manner whatsoever, including Internet usage, without written permission from Llewellyn Publications, except in the case of brief quotations embodied in critical articles and reviews.

FIRST EDITION
First Printing, 2013

Book design by Bob Gaul
Cover art: Rocks © Ann Cunning/Botanica/Getty Images
        Amethyst and Crystal Wand © iStockphoto.com/CreativeFire
Cover design by Ellen Lawson
Editing by Laura Graves
Interior illustrations © Llewellyn Art Department

Llewellyn Publications is a registered trademark of Llewellyn Worldwide Ltd.

Library of Congress Cataloging-in-Publication Data (Pending)
978-0-7387-3030-1

Llewellyn Worldwide Ltd. does not participate in, endorse, or have any authority or responsibility concerning private business transactions between our authors and the public.
   All mail addressed to the author is forwarded, but the publisher cannot, unless specifically instructed by the author, give out an address or phone number.
   Any Internet references contained in this work are current at publication time, but the publisher cannot guarantee that a specific location will continue to be maintained. Please refer to the publisher's website for links to authors' websites and other sources.

Llewellyn Publications
A Division of Llewellyn Worldwide Ltd.
2143 Wooddale Drive
Woodbury, MN 55125-2989
www.llewellyn.com

Printed in the United States of America

Acknowledgments

Writers never truly work alone. Special thanks to Louise and Ellen for their assistance during this project—rock shopping is always more fun with friends! Thanks to Elysia Gallo for her support and advice on the manuscript; and thanks to my mom and grandma for nurturing my childhood fascination with rocks. And, finally, to everyone who has ever given me a stone picked up on their travels around the world—thank you, and keep 'em coming!

Contents

Introduction

Do you remember the first time you gazed upon a crystal or faceted gemstone and were mesmerized by its sparkle? I, too, have a passion for stones: from the pure polished diamond of a wedding ring to the giant granite boulders that grace the landscape of my Midwestern home. I have felt the power of Earth while standing awestruck in the shadow of mountains and by contemplating tiny grains of sand. This is where the magic of stones begins—the way they inspire us, comfort us, and arouse a sense of wonder about the earth. Perhaps you have used a worry stone to soothe anxiety or felt more confident wearing a particular crystal pendant. If so, you know the power of crystal magic, and I invite you to continue your journey here.

My interest in rocks and minerals was the first step in my discovery of crystal magic. I remember finding a bit of pyrite when I was a child—of course I quickly learned it wasn't real gold, but this knowledge did little to dampen my enthusiasm or decrease my fascination.

Fossils also stirred my curiosity about the earth itself and the life that once walked upon it. I recall spending hours outside searching for rocks and studying them, amazed by form, sparkle, color—wanting to know why, where, and how.

I bought my first field guide when I was about ten years old; I still remember walking around with a magnifying glass trying to identify every specimen I collected. I also remember the first rock tumbler I had, grinding away in the basement, polishing stones. I had boxes of rocks stashed in the barn and in my bedroom. I had no idea this hobby would become so meaningful to my life, my love of nature eventually becoming a spiritual path.

We make meaning with our experiences. Stones may be surrounded by myth and folklore, but we can add to that knowledge and bring our own meaning and perspective to crystal magic. The spells in this book are designed to enhance your current knowledge of crystal magic and perhaps to offer new ways of working with stones that will help you continue your practice.

About the Spells

For the spells and rituals in this book, use whatever method you choose for creating sacred space or casting a circle. Assuming readers already have a basic understanding of magical timing and appropriate moon phases and moon signs, these details are not always given for each spell. In addition, begin all spells with stones that have been appropriately cleansed and charged—chapter one offers some techniques; in some cases, this method is part of the spell. Otherwise, use whatever method you prefer to prepare your stone(s).

The spells that follow are presented in chapters organized by style. For example, the section on preparation contains procedures for cleansing, charging, and dedicating stones; there's a chapter on jewelry, talismans, and amulets; one for stones in the home and garden; and other categories such as glass and sand, elixirs, and grids. You may progress through the chapters in order or jump around based on your interest.

In addition, the appendix contains lists and correspondences based on planetary associations, chakras, elements, and more. You can use this information to create your own crystal magic or locate a substitute stone if you don't have the one specifically called for in a spell.

You'll notice that all the spells in this book contain rhyming chants. This is because words help bring our intent into the physical realm— we are stating our purpose out loud to the universe. While the actual words don't contain power, they are one more tool we have in magical practice. Rhyming and rhythm also help the mind focus; sometimes the rhyme schemes and number of lines in a chant are based on numerology. Feel free to add your own words if you need to be more specific. As for any spell, the chants should be accompanied with visualization techniques—hopefully, the words will help with your visualization.

I use the word "stones" throughout this book to refer to all types of materials, including crystals and minerals, organic gems (substances from living organisms), metals, and rocks—the goal is to expand the realm of what we consider "crystal magic" to include these items. The ancient Greeks gave us the word crystal, *krystallos,* which means "ice," since clear quartz was once believed to be frozen water that couldn't melt. The scientific definition of a crystal is a mineral with specific atomic symmetry; a structure that repeats in an orderly pattern of units. Minerals are crystalline solids—atoms arranged in lattice structures with definite geometric patterns in a variety of chemical combinations. It is this special orderly structure that rests at the core of crystal magic. That being said, we should not ignore stones that lack a perfect crystalline structure, such as resins like amber, and even glass. You may notice I don't mention coral or ivory—this is because these particular organic (that is, from living organisms) "gems" are often rare or even endangered. Coral, especially the red variety, has long been used in jewelry; sadly, coral reefs are threatened around the world, and red coral has been severely overharvested. Ivory, too, should not be sought. Uses for amber, jet, and pearl are explored in this book, on the other hand.

If you practice crystal healing, please be aware that it is not necessarily the same as crystal magic. They may overlap in some areas, but this book primarily addresses using crystals and stones for their metaphysical properties in spells and rituals. To make the distinction, I like to think of crystal healing as affecting physical health and some emotional ailments, while crystal magic works more on the self and in a broader range of aspects—including one's environment. Again, these practices do overlap, and some methods of magic in this book will explore "internal" magic, especially by working to make change in oneself.

You probably already know that quartz (also referred to as rock crystal) is one of the most abundant minerals in the earth. It's made up of silicon and oxygen and has been used for more than a century in the electronics industry due to its piezoelectric effect. The metaphysical use of crystals raises the question: if crystals can be used to transmit radio signals, couldn't they also channel subtle energies to our bodies? And couldn't this affect us on many levels—spiritually, physically, and emotionally? Our bodies are energy, after all. And since magic involves using energy, crystals are just one more component to accessing the connection between ourselves and the universe, allowing us to make change in our lives.

By the time this book is printed, I will have been collecting rocks and minerals for almost thirty years. I still have many of the stones I collected as a child, and they hold memories of my experiences and explorations. I continue to collect and be inspired by stones, and I enjoy them both scientifically and metaphysically. When you see a perfect, natural crystal, you see the wonder of the universe itself—of atoms in order, a lovely balance. Is this an accident? Some divine plan? It doesn't matter. It's amazing, this symmetry and connection. We're all made of chemicals and arranged matter. It's important to keep that sense of awe and wonder alive as you practice crystal magic.

– ONE –

PREPARATION
FOR CRYSTAL MAGIC

Introduction

As with any magical technique, there are preparations that need to be made both for the tools and for the practitioner. Your stones and your state of mind must be clear and focused. It's tempting to simply rinse the stones quickly and begin, but I think you'll find it's worth the effort to make time for cleansing and charging—the very act will eventually become a trigger for your magical awareness.

You've heard the terms "cleansing" and "charging" before, and you probably already practice these techniques. And I'm sure you understand why you do it—cleansing rids an item of unwanted energy and charging (or programming) is used to project your intent onto an object. Often these words are used interchangeably, so I would like to offer some clarification. In this chapter you will find specific rituals for cleansing, charging, programming, and dedicating your stones, as well as detailed definitions of these terms.

Cleansing and Charging: Defined and Demystified

Cleansing can be both a literal cleaning of a stone and the removal (clearing) of other "energy" it may have been exposed to. The practical cleaning of a stone is a good idea for many reasons—the main reason is to remove dust and dirt. Plus, in a way, you're making the item your own by way of symbolic cleansing. Clearing of energy is a bit more intangible. Most practitioners of magic and other metaphysical arts believe that items can pick up energy from other sources and hold it for some time; this is why cleansing your stones is an excellent idea and a perfect first step when you acquire a new one. I like the use of the word *cleansing* to include both the literal and metaphysical cleaning of a stone—it implies a sense of renewal so the object is ready to be used for a new purpose.

Charging or programming is more difficult to define. The idea is that you can, and should, give your stone a focus before you use it—you define its purpose based on your intent and then use the stone as a tool to focus that intent in spells and rituals. And when you're done, the charge eventually wears off or is "erased" by cleansing. Also, if you consistently program the same stone for the same purpose, you reinforce your intent so that each time you see that stone, you instantly feel the focus.

Some magical practitioners believe that when you charge or program a stone, you're inscribing your thoughts into the very essence of that material. If that imagery is what helps you focus your intent, visualizing your thoughts inscribing the stone, great. Do it. Use whatever method works for you.

For charging or programming, choose the visualization you're most comfortable with. I like to imagine connecting with the stone on a mineralogical level—we're both (more or less) made of minerals. I visualize making a connection with a particular stone for a specific purpose at a particular moment in time. I visualize this connection as a bond, linking my intent with the stone. There are many different ways to do this, and I will offer some methods here—of course, feel free to create any way that works best for you. And, of course, you don't have to use the same method every time (although some people find that consistency helps with focus and intent).

The process of dedicating implies that you intend to use the stone over and over again with the same charge or program. Dedication can be essential, especially for a stone or piece of jewelry that you know you're going to use consistently for the same purpose. This is because the action helps the mind focus—and the mind is the seat of magical intent. This process is part of the aspect of ritual that draws us to magic. These actions are carried out with meaning that help us focus our intent and announce our purpose. Here's the way I break it down:

Cleansing: Washing away physical impurities and also a symbolic cleansing, marking the stone as being refreshed and renewed. This act removes unwanted energy from the stone using visualization and other techniques, often combined with physical cleaning. I use the word *cleansing* to refer to this combined process—cleaning and clearing of energy.

Charging/Programming and Dedicating: Charging and programming really mean the same thing—you charge a stone with specific intent for use in a spell or ritual; you dedicate a piece that you plan to use again and again for the same goal (or in a permanent talisman, piece of jewelry, or amulet). Dedication is simply repeated use of a stone for the same purpose. This can happen by charging the same piece over and over again, or by using a specific dedication ritual (or both).

Should you cleanse the stone immediately after the spell? It depends. I do cleanse stones before using them again; the timing is up to you. It mainly depends on the energy you're generating with the spell or ritual—you may not want to think of that energy lingering around. Or, you may want it to, if it's for a prosperity spell, for example. Crystal healers always cleanse and clear stones before and after use, so if you already practice this you may wish to use the same routine for your magical work.

Cleansing Methods

Not all cleansing methods should be used with all stones. Soft stones should never be soaked in water, and stones that have the tendency to crack or fade should never be charged in sunlight. Remember to use visualization techniques during the process. See the stone being cleared or erased, like a chalkboard, ready to receive your intent. These techniques are intended to remove unwanted energy from the stone. I have included a chant to use for each method. To save time, you may wish to cleanse multiple stones together.

For practical cleansing—removal of dirt or dust—clean your stone with gentle hand soap or toothpaste using cool or lukewarm water. For clusters, use an old toothbrush or cotton swab to reach between all the crevices. Dry with a soft towel or let the stone air-dry. This method also works for jewelry—of course, you may wish to use a special jewelry cleaner instead or a cloth designed to remove tarnish from metals.

Elemental

As the name suggests, this method uses the four classical elements of Earth, Air, Fire, and Water to cleanse the stone. You will need something to represent each: a dish of soil, a burning candle, burning incense, and a dish of water.

METHOD:

Dip the stone in the water, then pass the stone quickly through the flame (don't burn your fingers!). Next, pass the stone through the incense smoke, and, finally, place the stone in the dish of soil.

As you perform each task, visualize that element removing any unwanted energy from the stone: Water renews and washes away; Fire burns; Air blows; Earth absorbs.

CHANT:

Water, Fire, Air, and Earth,
Cleanse this stone, give rebirth.

Smudging

This method uses smoke from incense or burning herbs to dispel negative energy and purify the object. The most traditional choices are sagebrush or frankincense, but use what you like best. You can hold the stone in your hand and pass it through the smoke, or place the stone on a table or other type of stand and allow the smoke to drift over it. I like to use a tall candle holder designed for a pillar or taper candle. Most stones will fit on top and then you can place the incense below or beside it, allowing the smoke to drift over the stone for a longer period of time.

CHANT:

Smolder, smoke, blow away,
Cleanse this stone, clear the way.

Water

When cleansing with water, it's nice to use water collected from a natural spring or spring-fed stream. If you don't have access to this, use distilled water or plain tap water if you'd like. You can even make a special cleansing elixir (see chapter four). You can allow the stone to soak in the water for a period of time in sunlight, moonlight, by candlelight, or you can rinse the stone under running water. It's up to you, and you may find that your preference often depends on the stone's intended use. Some people like to use salt water, which is fine as long as the stone you're cleansing isn't too soft.

CHANT:
Rushing water running clear,
old intention disappear.

Water cleanse and clear this stone,
until its future purpose known.

Sunlight or Moonlight

Simply place the stone where it can sit in sunlight or moonlight for an extended period of time. You may wish to use this in combination with water cleansing; rinse the stone, then use light to complete the process.

CHANT:
Sunlight/Moonlight, as you cleanse this stone,
By your light make it my own

Earth Cleansing

Place the stone in a container of soil for 24 hours.

CHANT:
Soil of the Earth, renew this stone's true worth.

Music and Sounds

Sounds can be utilized for cleansing by ringing a bell, or using a gong or singing bowl. Sing these lines or chant while you make sounds or play music:

> *As this sound does reach my ear,*
> *I declare this stone is clear.*

Salt

As described in the water cleansing method, you can use salt water for some stones. A bed of coarse sea salt crystals is also an excellent choice for cleansing. Allow the stone to sit on the salt overnight, throughout the day, or for a 24-hour period.

CHANT:
Purify and clear this stone;
Its intent shall be my own.

Using Quartz Clusters or Other Stones

Allowing a stone or piece of jewelry to rest on a large cluster of clear quartz is one of the easiest methods of cleansing. Kyanite is also a good mineral to use for clearing energy from other stones. Allow the stone to remain on the clearing crystal(s) for at least 24 hours.

CHANT:
Stone on stone, neutralize,
Clear away all prior ties.

Charging and Dedicating

Charging (or programming) is the term used for establishing temporary intent—for example, you use a piece of amethyst for a restful sleep spell, and later cleanse it and charge it to use for meditation. Perhaps you use a piece of tiger eye for a prosperity spell, and use it again in the future for a grounding ritual. This method of cleansing and charging over and over again is perfectly fine.

However, you may wish to keep a particular stone or piece of jewelry for one purpose. In this case, use dedication—your intent to use this piece permanently (or for an extended period of time) for a singular purpose—a protective amulet, for example, or a crystal ball for divination.

Methods of Charging and Dedicating

The most important thing to remember when charging is to clearly visualize your intent. See what you want; focus on your goal. Ideally, you'll use the same (or a similar) visualization during the spell or ritual to reinforce your intent. Hold the stone in your projective hand during the charging process or hold your projective hand over the stone(s). It may help you to speak your intent aloud or even write it down on paper and place the stone on top. If you have several stones to use for a spell, you can charge them together, even if they serve slightly different purposes. They will be united by your goal in the spell.

Also, remember to consider your need; your goal with a spell may be general or specific. For example, rather than focusing on general prosperity, you can focus on your specific need, such as paying off debts or making more money. You could also use a visualization where you can see yourself in the situation you desire. In some situations, you need to remain general and open, such as when seeking love. Don't neglect how you might limit yourself—think of it kind of like surfing the Internet: when you're doing a search, sometimes you need to be very specific but other times you want all options revealed to you.

ALL-PURPOSE CHARGING CHANT:
Now I focus my intent
Hear me as my goal is sent.
I connect it to this stone
Making my true purpose known.
Let this tool now work with me
As I will so shall it be.

State your purpose for the spell. To dedicate, add these lines:

With this chant let all be told
Let this dedication hold.

Other Methods

Just as sounds can be used to clear energy, they can help with programming and dedicating as well. Play a particular type of music when you're visualizing your intent. You will come to associate this sound with that stone and your purpose. You can also use bells, singing bowls, drums, or other instruments.

If you work with essential oils, you may wish to add a few drops of oil to a carrier solution and apply this to a crystal. Again, use caution that the stone won't be damaged. Choose a scent associated with your purpose, and you'll be reminded of your goal each time you detect that particular aroma.

Dedicating Crystal Clusters

Most people I know who collect stones for any reason are fascinated by clusters. They seem to be a world of their own, like a mountain range, a world you could get lost in. Some have more crystals that you can count. And they sparkle like no other natural form. They make lovely decorative pieces and they're excellent for magic.

Magically, clusters are often used to create a sense of community or harmony in a room, or during group magical practice. They also make beautiful symbols for the center of an altar.

Here's a chant you can use to dedicate a cluster for a general peaceful environment.

Crystal cluster represent
harmony and good intent;
peacefulness upon this space
by every shining crystal face.

You will also find clusters of other varieties of quartz and other minerals as well. The meanings for those will correspond to the meaning of the mineral. For example, a cluster of amethyst might be used to enhance the spiritual atmosphere; citrine would be useful for a harmonious and successful work environment. Whatever the mineral, think of the cluster as having an extra boost of energy specially tailored for a community or group.

EXAMPLES:

- A clear quartz cluster with several points that appear to be self-healed would be good in an environment where healing and comfort are needed.

- A smoky quartz cluster could be used for balance and temperance within a group setting, such as trying to overcome a bad habit or other obstacle.

- A cluster of apophyllite or amethyst would be good to use for psychic or magical work in a group, or in a group's remote work.

These are excellent for individual work as well, since a cluster is visually stunning and appealing. Placing one in a room can help you with individual needs—visualize the energy being projected all around you, from every point of the cluster.

Centering and Grounding

These are important aspects of magical work with which you are undoubtedly familiar—though perhaps they are confusing. If you find the process challenging, you may wish to dedicate specific stones to always use for centering and grounding. Remember, repeated use for the same purpose over time is a kind of automatic dedication. This dedication process may help you form a method for reaching these desired states. Here are some suggestions for these practices using stones.

Centering Ritual

To be centered means to be balanced physically, spiritually, and in all the subtle bodies as well. This concept is a bit intangible—most of us simply know the feeling when we reach it. To use stones to aid centering, select those used for meditation, to stimulate the mind, and those recommended for spirituality. Clear fluorite is a good choice for this task, and clear quartz is always appropriate. In addition, hematite is one of those rare stones that are good for both centering and grounding. Hold the stone(s) while you meditate, practice breathing exercises, or use sound (music, bells). You can also gaze at stones and practice centering this way. In addition, using prayer beads can help one become centered and focused.

CHANT:

Body, mind, and spirit now align,
center, focus on this goal of mine;
subtle bodies balanced to the core,
Clear and strong I'm ready to explore.

This chant can help create a sense of connectedness:

To the sky, spirit rise
lift my voice, lift my eyes,
See the sun, moon, and stars,
Touch them all, mine and ours.

Grounding Ritual

When you are well-grounded, you are cleared of excess energy. You are properly connected (think of a power cord), so any excess energy flows into the earth. Lack of grounding during magical practice can result in nervousness, restlessness, short temper, fatigue, and even illness (since you may be exhausted and your immune system might weaken). Other symptoms are dizziness, an unbalanced feeling, being confused, chakra imbalances, and subtle energy disturbances in the aura or other subtle bodies.

To select stones for grounding, think "heavy"—especially metallic ores like lodestone, galena, and hematite. Bronzite and barite ("desert rose") are less commonly used but are both heavy and also good choices for grounding. Dark-colored stones like black tourmaline, smoky quartz, and onyx can also be used. Experiment with several to see which ones feel right for you. Hold the stone in your hands, cupping one palm inside the other. A popular visualization for grounding is to imagine yourself as a tree, roots digging into the soil. You can also visualize yourself as a stone.

CHANT:

To the ground, I am bound,
see my roots reaching down,
feel the weight of the stone,
one with Earth, flesh and bone.

The Mundane Stuff: Shopping for Stones

The discussion of preparation would not be complete without a few words on obtaining stones. Nearly everyone who works with stones for magic knows these items can be purchased at a variety of shops and various online outlets. In addition, don't overlook gem and mineral shows, if these events occur in your area. I have found these to be an ideal place to find raw and tumbled stones, supplies, and jewelry. In some cases you avoid the "middle man" at these shows and purchase directly from a supplier—plus, there are no shipping costs.

When you attend a gem and mineral show, there are different shopping approaches you can take. If you're looking for something in particular, study the entire room first before you buy. Often dealers will have similar objects at very different prices. I recently saw three vendors with the same massage wands at three different prices—one had them for half the price of the others—and they were exactly the same. If you are simply browsing, walk in the room and let your intuition be your guide, leading you to what you need. Of course, if you feel "drawn" to something or an overwhelming urge to buy a stone, you should probably listen to your inner voice.

I was once looking specifically for a clear quartz sphere, the "classic" crystal ball. The first vendor I approached had two, both reasonably priced. One was clearly of better quality than the other, and it was exactly what I was looking for. My mind said I should look around first, so I started to walk away. But then, my intuition kicked in and said—you should buy it now! So I did. And it's a good thing, because no other vendor at the event had clear quartz spheres I could afford; still, years later, I have yet to see another of equal quality for the price I paid.

You may buy stones you're attracted to for no apparent reason only to research them later and realize you have a need for them at that moment in your life. Or you may simply want a pretty piece for your collection. Don't you love it when you unexpectedly find something that you need but weren't actively looking for? This often happens when you intuitively shop for stones. (Chapter eight explores personal power stones in detail.)

Be aware that there are often many types of vendors at these events—jewelry suppliers, stone cutters, metaphysical store owners, geologists, and more. Some offer very nice pieces but you will undoubtedly encounter some poor quality items. Good mineral specimens are usually accompanied by an information card of some kind bearing the location where it was found, or the information is displayed near the items. A good dealer will be able to answer all your questions and will be honest about synthetic pieces. I once found a piece that appeared to be tumbled cat's eye (cymophane) in with some other natural stones that were shaped into spheres. When I asked, I was told that the cat's eye was in fact fiber optic and not natural. Real cat's eye is quite rare and expensive.

The more you know about minerals, the better shopper you will be. If you know a stone is common or rare, for example, you can be a better judge of the price. You may encounter some overpriced pieces, but you can also find some very good deals. When in doubt about identifying a stone, ask. Most vendors are avid collectors, often investing a lifetime of study into minerals—they know what they're doing. And most of them, like us, have a passion for rocks.

- TWO -

Jewelry, Amulets, and Talismans

Introduction

We love to decorate our bodies, and jewelry is the easiest nonpermanent way. Magical jewelry is more than decoration—it serves a purpose. One could speculate that the very origin of wearing jewelry began with wearing stones as protective amulets or talismans, or to attract good fortune. It seems that despite the various differences in the meaning of stones across cultures, they have been used universally throughout history as protective symbols.

This chapter includes spells for items that are worn or carried, hidden or in plain view. Often there is a fine line between magical jewelry, talismans, and amulets. First of all, there is a subtle difference between a talisman and an amulet. By definition, a talisman is an item that is carried or worn for a specific purpose, usually to attract something (such as wealth or good fortune). An amulet is carried or worn for a general purpose, usually to repel something (evil), thus giving protection. Often you will see these words used interchangeably.

In ancient times, talismans were often stones that contained an engraving, word, or symbol; an amulet was a stone placed inside a small pouch or bag, along with a written phrase or invocation. Amulets were used to ward off danger and protect the wearer from poison, animals, enemies, and so on. Talismans were used to draw good fortune, love, health, wealth, and power.

Naturally, an amulet or talisman can be a piece of jewelry. For example, say you have a troublesome coworker, an oppressive boss, a family member you argue with, or a rude neighbor. Wear a visible amulet when dealing with those people. Sometimes it's nice if this piece is bold and not subtle. A large locket or ring can be quite impressive. A brooch works nicely, too. Here's my general rule: a bundle is for hiding; jewelry should be seen (of course, there are exceptions). If it looks powerful, it will feel more powerful when you wear it. However, if you do want to be subtle, make sure the piece fits with your outfit and just looks like an accessory. Make sure it fits your style and doesn't look out of place.

I realize there may be certain situations where wearing a particular symbol, such as a pentacle, may draw unwanted attention. Wearing jewelry under your clothing is always an option. But sometimes you can find ways around this. One idea is to wear a piece of magical jewelry with subtle symbolism that will go unnoticed or seem merely decorative—a secret hidden in plain sight. For example, a pentacle woven among Celtic knots or the image of an animal or tree that holds special significance for you. A dolphin pendant can be just a pendant or a representation of one's animal totem. You can even wear a simple locket that contains bits of magical herbs or a ring that has special symbols engraved inside the band. And since semiprecious gemstone jewelry is popular and found in mainstream stores, it doesn't look out of place to wear an amethyst pendant, for example, or a big chunk of amber. Classic pieces of stone jewelry are always fashionable.

Love Pendant

This spell is for taking a risk in love, as we so often do. This will not prevent you from being heartbroken; it is intended to give you strength and self-love so when or if heartbreak happens, you will be strong. If you're searching for love, dating someone, or you've just realized a dating relationship is becoming more intimate, try this pendant. Focus on self-love and the knowledge that it comes first in any relationship. You can't love others if you don't love yourself.

STONES:

- Find a heart-shaped piece of rose quartz that can be worn as a pendant.

- You will also need enough malachite chips to form a small circle around the rose quartz.

- Alternate option: Make a necklace with the rose quartz heart pendant and string malachite beads along with it.

First, build a circle of malachite stones around the heart—if you have a string of malachite chips that can be worn as a necklace that would be an ideal choice. Malachite is associated with the heart chakra and is a protective stone. The rose quartz will be the piece you will end up wearing, unless you make the necklace combination. If you don't have a piece of rose quartz that is heart-shaped, or one you can wear, use a rough or tumbled piece that you can carry. Ultimately, you will wear or carry the rose quartz so it rests against your chest, near the heart chakra.

When you're ready, visualize and chant:

I give my heart, my love is strong
Even if it all goes wrong;
I believe, my heart is brave
No matter what, my heart is saved.

Ring Around Your Wrist—A Reminder Spell

You're probably familiar with the concept of tying a string around your finger to help you remember something. This spell works along this same principle: wear something that keeps you from forgetting. I like bracelets, but often find them annoying after wearing them for a while. However, this works well if I'm trying to keep my mind on something such as, for example, trying to break a bad habit. Let's say you want to stop an unconscious habit of biting your fingernails. Dedicate a bracelet for this purpose and each time you lift your hand to do the deed, you'll remember not to. Very simple. I like to use a bracelet that has charms or beads dangling from it. For a very specific spell, choose stone beads and create a bracelet suited just for your purpose. Burn a candle in the center of the bracelet to charge it, and use this chant to seal the spell:

Ring around my wrist on cue,
Help me to remember true.
Bind me to the task at hand,
To my goal I latch this band.

When the candle burns out, begin wearing the bracelet. Charge it again anytime you feel it's necessary.

Amber Spells for Attraction

One of the many attributes of amber is that it's said to make its wearer irresistible. The stone has an irresistible appeal itself—soft and glowing, warm like a sunset. The medium orange color is the most popular and the type that is best used in these spells. Be sure you have real amber and not a synthetic imitation—amber is easily falsified using plastic. To test your amber, rub the piece briskly with a scrap of velvet. You may have to do this several times to work up an electrical charge. Real amber will attract tiny bits of lint or paper; plastic will not.

Based on its color, amber is often associated with the sun or the element of Fire but, by origin, amber is more properly connected to the Earth element. Since amber is fossilized resin from trees, it has the "earthy" qualities that nurture us. Perform these spells on a Friday and, if you wish, call on Aphrodite, Venus, or Freya to assist you. Remember: to the Greeks, Aphrodite was a goddess of physical love, not emotional love. If you call on her or on Venus, her Roman counterpart, be aware of this aspect of her personality. In addition, you can use these spells any day (waxing or full moon phase is best) if you feel the need.

Remember, you aren't directing this energy at others; rather, you're affecting yourself, looking and feeling your best, and enhancing the natural qualities you possess that attract people to you. Try to avoid focusing on controlling the way others see you—work on yourself, and what you project. There are several types of spells here—combine them if you'd like.

These spells use jewelry because it's easy to wear and most people feel that accessories like jewelry can add a particular appeal to their physical appearance. Carrying a piece of the stone with you may not be as effective. There's a special magic in seeing the piece of jewelry interacting with the energy and personality of the wearer. However, if you wish to be more subtle, or for any reason can't wear jewelry or don't have any, you can carry a piece of amber instead. Keep it in your purse, briefcase, or pocket. Or, use this spell in conjunction with the Talisman for Success and carry the bundle with you. There may be moments when you want to be appealing, but being too appealing could be a disadvantage.

The goal here is to achieve attention that will get you noticed in various ways. Perhaps you have a job interview and want to make a positive impression—use a spell to boost your best qualities. Each spell is designed to be fairly gentle, but you can increase the power by the way you charge your specific piece. You can use a spell to help you gain that second glance from someone you'd like to meet or to give you confidence by putting your best features forward. That's why there are so many variations of this attraction spell.

The main requirement is a piece (or two) of amber jewelry. Don't go overboard! I have four amber necklaces, a pair of earrings, a bracelet, and two rings—but I'd never wear them all at once. But, if you have a matching set with necklace, earrings, bracelet and ring, go ahead and combine them in the way you feel is most attractive. Keep in mind that while it's expected your lovely jewelry will be noticed, you want people to notice you as well—not just your jewelry. Perhaps for a casual look, the only piece of jewelry you wear is a very small but stunning amber pendant which accents your neckline. That would be enough. Or, for a dressy style, try a large pendant on a long chain with a matching ring or bracelet. Use your own sense of style as a guide. To be on the conservative side, perhaps for a job interview, you may just want a small ring or a bundle to hide (combine with Talisman for Success).

First, charge a piece of amber jewelry for the type of attraction you desire—be careful: you could get exactly what you wish for! Some kinds of attention may be unwanted.

The enchantment on the jewelry piece will eventually wear off, so recharge it each time you need it. However, using the same stone repeatedly for the same purpose will dedicate it for ease of use.

Always remember to visualize your best self and project that image, along with a positive attitude. You must also act in the mundane world to support your magic. You can't expect success with these spells if you don't pay attention to the details of your personal grooming habits, appearance, and behavior.

Cleanse your jewelry first. For each spell, unless otherwise specified, hold the item in your projective hand while you visualize your specific purpose and chant.

FOR A GENERAL POSITIVE APPEARANCE:

Use this spell to attract general positive energy and help things go your way.

Help me to project my best
Qualities that I possess.
Favor me with special glance,
Grant me this distinctive chance.

FOR PHYSICAL BEAUTY—YOUR BEST TRAITS:

This spell is intended to help your best physical traits draw attention.

Gentle amber from the tree,
You have aged so beautifully.
This I ask respectfully,
Let others see the best of me.

TO CATCH SOMEONE'S EYE:

There are many ways to stand out in a crowd—some of which place people in unfavorable light. This spell is intended to get you noticed, but in a subtle way. What is seen after that depends on you. This spell will not change anything about you, but is designed for your best attributes to stand out and for you not only to be seen, but to be seen favorably.

CHANT:
Amber now lend me your glow.
Let my real beauty show.
May all/his/her eyes now favor me,
For good of all so mote it be.

ATTRACTION SPELL FOR A SPECIFIC PERSON:
While it's not a good idea to try and bend anyone's free will, this is a "safe" spell to see if the person you desire shares your interest. Try it, and watch for subtle signs. If the one you seek does not appear to notice you, don't force it. Never try to manipulate someone to fall in love with you—your actions will undoubtedly backfire. Chant three times:

Draw him/her to me, moth to flame,
Only if he/she feels the same.
Without force and without harm,
Gently now I cast this charm.

This spell is meant to help you discover if the attraction is mutual; it's not intended to speed up a relationship or change the way someone feels about you. You can also combine this with the Eye Catching spell for a boost to get noticed.

Ring Spells

Rings are one of the oldest forms of jewelry. Greek mythology names Prometheus as the first ring-wearer. He was pardoned by Zeus for his crime of stealing fire and giving it to humans, but he was sentenced to wear an iron ring set with a stone from the rock he had been chained to during his original punishment. Symbolically, even after he was physically freed from his bond, he would remain "chained" forever. Rings are most often used to represent a bond—such as wedding rings, class rings, and so on. They have also been used to symbolize perfection, attainment, and everlasting life due to their never-ending circle.

Rings seem to be among the most popular forms of jewelry of magical practitioners, both for simple adornment and as magical or ritual objects. Necklaces and pendants are probably just as popular, but in my experience there's something especially powerful about seeing the rings on your fingers, probably since we so often work with our hands in magic.

RING FOR HEALTH AND VITALITY:

In this case, find a ring set with one of the following stones: agate, lapis lazuli, tiger eye, garnet, or topaz. Cleanse the ring by both cleaning it of any physical dirt or tarnish and then placing it in a glass of water in the sunlight for a few hours. Visualize the sun warming the water and this healing light penetrating the stone. Note: Do not use this method with lapis! It's a soft stone. Just rinse it with water and then set it in the sun for no more than an hour.

CHANT:

Light of life, grant to me, warm and vibrant energy.

Dry the ring and hold it in your projective hand. Visualize and chant again. Next, perform the ritual. Place the ring on your receptive hand. Dance—see yourself at your most perfect, your peak of health and beauty, your most vibrant. Feel it. Know that when you need a boost you can wear this ring and it will help you feel energized. Capture your most radiant feeling within the stone. When you wear this ring, it will give you energy.

"Everyday" Magic Ring:

If you have a favorite ring that you wear every day, you can dedicate it for a magical purpose. Cleanse your ring and hold it in your projective hand to charge and/or dedicate it for your purpose. Visualize your needs and goals. Depending on the type of stone in your ring, you may decide on a specific type of charging method such as sunlight or moonlight. Use this chant to focus your intent:

Sparkle, shine, stone of mine,
Grant the need that I define.

State your purpose.

Ring for Success:

Good choices for this ring are citrine or tiger eye. Both stones are related to the Fire element and can be used to draw success and prosperity. This is also a good choice for an everyday ring since success is often something we cultivate in our lives each day and drawing this positive quality is a good reminder of our goals and potential.

Tiger eye is grounding and wealth-oriented, and it is also used for protection and strength. The beautiful golden-brown of tiger eye is a perfect symbol for the rich earth, even though it's associated with the Fire element. The shimmering bands glow and shine in the light like an internal fire—think of this as representing your inner glow and strength.

Citrine is better suited for purposes of general success and optimism, clarity, or specifically for business or education. In cut gemstone form, citrine is usually yellow and dazzling like a bit of sunshine—cheerful and optimistic—a symbol of success.

Generally, your projective hand is the one you write with—used to project energy outward. Your receptive hand draws things to you. In this case, either hand can be used. For example, you want to project an attitude of success and optimism, but you also want to draw those qualities to you. If you can't decide, try each and see if you prefer one over the other. This is not a hard and fast rule.

Cleanse your ring gently with water and allow it to sit in sunshine to dry. When you're ready to proceed, hold the ring and meditate on your purpose—success, wealth, or a combination of both. Light a white or yellow candle on your altar and place the ring beside it. Visualize the flame of the candle infusing the ring with energy.

CHANT:

With this ring, pledge success,
Show the skills that I possess.
Let me shine, let me glow,
With this ring, wealth I know.

Let the candle burn out. Recharge the ring by repeating the spell whenever you feel it's necessary.

VARIATION:

Wear a tiger eye ring on your receptive hand to attract wealth and a citrine ring on your projective hand to project an attitude of success.

Protection Amulet

This amulet is a bundle to be carried with you, so be sure to use a small stone. Create this amulet during a waxing or full moon phase.

STONES:

One of the following, depending on your specific need:

- **clear quartz**: all-purpose

- **tiger eye**: courage

- **black tourmaline or obsidian:** repelling unwanted energy

- **garnet:** guards against thieves (good to keep in a vehicle)

- **turquoise:** protection during a spiritual journey

- **moonstone:** protection during travel

OTHER ITEMS:
- Incense (frankincense, if possible)

- A candle of any size, white or red

- A piece of red or white cloth for wrapping the stone
  (or a drawstring bag)

- String, ribbon, or twine

Create sacred space as desired. Light the incense and the candle. Pass the stone through the incense smoke and chant:

Rising smoke, clear this stone.

Next (holding the stone safely in tongs, if you wish), charge it by passing it quickly through the candle flame and chant:

Rising flame, charge this stone.

Hold the stone in your projective hand and wrap your fingers around it. Focus your intent on your specific need. Speak it out loud if you'd like. Chant five times:

Stone as guard, danger barred:
To protect, none detect.

Wrap the fabric around the stone and tie it in a knot with the ribbon or string. Allow the wrapped stone to rest near the candle until it burns out. Allow the incense to burn out as well.

Carry the amulet with you in your pocket, handbag, briefcase, backpack, etc., for as long as you feel the need. Recharge the amulet as you feel is necessary.

Talisman to Relieve Tension

Use this spell for a situation in which you need to be alert and relaxed at the same time, such as a presentation, job interview, or an exam—any tense situation (even a first date) where you still want to have sharp mental focus. Or, you can use this spell as a meditation to help you find your direction or during a waiting period where you feel your destiny unfolding. For this spell, you can carry a loose stone or wear it set in jewelry—preferably silver. In addition, consider meditating with a tumbled piece. Perform when the moon is Scorpio or Pisces.

You will need a piece of labradorite that is tumbled, set in jewelry, or both. Labradorite is a beautiful member of the feldspar group, similar to moonstone. Labradorite is the plagioclase variety and is named for the location where it was discovered—Labrador, Canada. This stone can help reduce stress and anxiety. It protects and balances the aura, aids in understanding one's destiny, enhances patience, perseverance, and inner knowing. It can give you discernment in direction; you'll be able to "know the right time." (This spell can be combined with the Talisman for Success.) Associated with the moon, it has a soft, feminine energy. It can help bring intuition into thought—useful when you need to think on your feet.

Select your desired piece(s), cleanse them, and prepare your space. Visualize your specific goal while you hold the stone or jewelry to charge it.

CHANT:

Insight sharp, calm of mind,
Focus on this place and time.
Balanced thought, at my best—
shining through, pass the test.

VARIATION:

You may wish to incorporate the following meditation, intended to be done either while waiting for the spell to manifest or in place of the spell—sometimes divination will tell you to be introspective rather than taking action. Other times, it will tell you that action you've already taken is still in progress. This meditation helps stabilize the energy and ensures that you remain calm, strong, and dedicated to the outcome. Alternately, if you're unsure about a situation, this meditation can help guide you. Use it along with divination.

CHANT:

Keep me patient as I wait,
With the guiding hand of Fate.
Here I linger at the gate,
Knowing what unfolds is great.

Talisman for Success

Create this talisman to carry any time you need to accomplish a goal or you're nearing the completion of something you've been working on. This talisman is especially good for job interviews, presentations, and exams. There is a variation you can use if the goal is a major life achievement or calling—your "dream" job, for example, or a presentation that holds a major life event or change in the balance.

Since this talisman is to be carried, choose stones of a manageable size. Perform this spell during a waxing moon, when the moon is in Taurus, Virgo, or Capricorn, if possible.

STONES:

- a small piece of amber

- a small piece of citrine quartz

- a piece of amber jewelry (optional, in case you want to wear it now or in the future)

OTHER ITEMS:

- Small pouch, preferably yellow

- a piece of devil's shoestring (herb, root of virburum)

- incense, candle, mirror (optional)

Place the stones and herb in the pouch and tie it securely. You may wish to burn a candle nearby or place the bundle on a mirror near a window where the sunlight can shine through. Burn appropriate incense as desired. Visualize your specific need and chant:

I will succeed, my goal is near.
I will succeed, my way is clear.
I will succeed, my time is here.

Carry the bundle with you.

VARIATION:

Add a piece of labradorite jewelry during the charging process (*see* Talisman to Relieve Tension). This stone can aid your efforts as well, especially when you are facing an opportunity that you believe is your destiny or a strong calling toward a life-goal. It adds strength and perseverance, as well as having a calming effect, similar to moonstone (they're both feldspars and can be used to promote self-awareness). It also helps transform intuition into intellectual information—it can serve as a bridge between mysticism and psychic ability, leading to understanding—knowing how to use this wisdom. Labradorite facilitates transformation and helps one know the "right" time. It allows one to transcend limitations and embrace the moment, and it gives confidence.

A friend of mine was wearing a labradorite pendant during a moment when she received a very important job. It was a part-time internship, but it was a position that enabled her to gain experience in her field of study and pursue her dream. When it came time for her to interview for a full-time position in the field, she wore the same pendant (and carried this talisman). In addition, she combined the talisman with an amber ring that she continued to wear during the decision-making process. And, yes, she got the job—and is now happily advancing in her career.

Talisman for Success in Legal Matters

Carry this talisman with you during any type of court case or situation involving other types of legal action such as fines or fees. A friend of mine carried it throughout her bankruptcy case, and everything worked out for the best—better than she could have hoped, in fact. Focus on the best possible outcome.

- A piece of grossular garnet, pale green (or orange) in color

- A small, clear quartz point (optional) to increase the garnet's energy

- A small drawstring bag in white or yellow

- Three fresh or dried yellow or orange marigold flowers

Place the stones and flowers inside the bag and draw the string. Tie it three times, and with each tie, say these words:

Success in this ordeal be mine,
resolve the issue in swift time.
The outcome here will favor me—
As I will, so shall it be.

Carry the talisman as needed until the issue is resolved—make sure you have it with you when meeting with lawyers, especially if you are required to appear in court. Ladies, I recommend keeping it in your purse; gentlemen, perhaps a briefcase or in your pocket.

Moonstone Travel Amulet

Moonstone is reputed to be "the traveler's stone." I use this amulet for any type of overnight travel, and even for very long day trips. For this spell, you will need three small pieces of moonstone—one to leave at home on your altar, one to carry with you, and another to keep in one of your bags. The one you carry can be in the form of jewelry, if you'd like (or use the three stones and add a piece of jewelry as well). I usually wear a ring in addition to one loose piece in a handbag I carry. The other one stays in my suitcase.

Dedicate all three pieces together. Visualize a bond between the stones, connecting you back to home, and keeping the connection during your trip. You can place them beside a candle, if you wish, or simply hold them while imagining a safe and enjoyable journey, seeing yourself back home again.

CHANT:

On this journey keep me safe by land or sky or sea,
Safe journey, safe return—So mote it be.

Leave one stone on the altar until you return. Keep one in a suitcase or travel bag, and carry the other in your pocket or purse.

Fluorite Spell for Focus

Fluorite does not have a long metaphysical history. In fact, it's considered by some to be a "New Age" stone. Because of its many colors and lovely formations, it definitely has a place in crystal magic. (And yes, it's the source of fluoride.) Metaphysically, fluorite promotes order and reason. It can help with concentration and meditation. According to the detailed reference book *Love is in the Earth*, it is a "stone of discernment and aptitude." Some have also called it "the genius stone."

Fluorite has a cubic internal structure (see the appendix for a complete explanation of crystal structure), and it is often found in lovely natural octahedron shapes (eight-sided). The octahedrons are especially good for promoting an orderly environment. To use the octahedrons, carry them in a protective pouch to prevent the points from chipping.

In addition, fluorite is often carved, especially into spheres and points—some of which display a gorgeous blending of violet, blue, and green shades. These are excellent meditation stones when carved, since they're smooth and comforting to hold. You may not find a great deal of fluorite jewelry on the market (it's not a very durable stone and is easily scratched), however, you can find fluorite beads to make your own jewelry. They're also sometimes found in carved points to be worn as pendants.

When you're feeling like life is particularly chaotic or it is difficult to focus or concentrate, use this spell. Any color of fluorite will work, but clear is the most general. However, to add an additional element of specificity to your spell, use a colored version based on its properties.

The octahedron is the best choice for this spell, but you may use a carved shape if that's all you have. Carry the stone with you, hold it during meditation, or keep it nearby on a desk or table. For each purpose that follows, cleanse the stone, then hold it while visualizing your goal and chanting:

CLEAR/GENERAL
Stone of order, calm my mind,
Bring me energy refined.

BLUE/COMMUNICATION
Help my message to be heard,
loud and clear, understood.

PURPLE/THIRD EYE
Give me insight that I need,
Information I should heed.

YELLOW/CREATIVITY
Inspiration for my art,
From my spirit and my heart.

GREEN/FRESHEN A SPACE
A space to work that's clean and clear,
No discomfort lingers here.

Talisman for Acceptance and Comfort

Unfortunately, loss is unavoidable. Whether it's loss of a loved one, a pet, a relationship, or even a job, we will all experience this at some time in our lives. While there's no spell or trinket that can truly ease the pain, sometimes simply acknowledging the grief can help us begin to accept it. For any situation where you need comfort or the ability to accept something (loss, grief, a broken heart, disappointment) make this talisman.

STONES:

- **Apache tear obsidian** provides an attitude of forgiveness and helps one accept grief—the Fire element helps you move forward.

- **Lepidolite** is a lovely transition stone—promotes self-love and is soothing to the emotions. It can also help you understand the root of your distress, if you're unsure. This stone adds the comfort of the Water element.

- **Optional:** Dolomite—eases sorrow and helps one to understand and accept.

Charge the stones by holding them and visualizing their qualities wrapping you like a comforting blanket. To make the bundle, place the stones in a white pouch and tie it with a white ribbon.

CHANT:
In my time of need and sorrow,
Help me look toward tomorrow.
If a lesson I must learn,
Help me know and to discern.
Comfort me here in the dark,
bring love and strength into my heart.

Citrine Spell to Clear the Way

This spell is intended to help eliminate barriers between you and your goal—primarily related to business, employment, or education. Citrine is not only a stone of success and prosperity, but it promotes communication and brings a positive influence to any situation. It's also a stone of optimism. The Fire element is utilized here for growth, movement, and change.

This spell can be cast simply by just using this one stone (or stone and cluster combination). It's simple and subtle so you can both carry a stone and keep one at home or in the workplace.

Maybe you're waiting for a promotion or to hear about a job you applied for; or you're hoping for a raise, but you're aware of some obstacles beyond your control. Perhaps you're waiting for paperwork to go through for a loan to start your own business. Or you're waiting to hear word about college—acceptance or financial aid. Anytime you feel blocked in the practical world, use this spell; it's especially good to begin during a waning moon phase.

You will need a small citrine quartz point. In addition, you may also incorporate a cluster of citrine, a piece you can have sitting near you at home or work. If you don't have a single citrine point or a cluster, use a piece of citrine jewelry or a tumbled stone.

You may wish to perform a divination before this spell to help you know how to proceed. Working magic like this is like working with people—sometimes you need to use finesse; sometimes you need to be more assertive—determine if you need to softly dissolve the barrier or break or burn it, even. This spell can be forceful, using the imagery of fire to burn through and transform (not literally, of course), or it can be a bit softer, when obstacles melt away. You get the idea. If you feel you need a gentler approach, use the alternate version.

Charge/Dedicate your stone(s) as you wish. Visualize your need or goal, and see the way being cleared. Since citrine is associated with the sun and Fire, imagine the crystal point sending a beam of fire to melt barriers that block your path to success. One reason a small cluster is a beneficial addition is that you can visualize the energy from all the points projecting many times. Hold the stone(s) in your projective hand as you chant and visualize. Carry the stone with you and place a cluster where you can see it in the environment of the desired goal.

If you happen to know what the obstacle is, specifically visualize it. If not, simply imagine that whatever could be in the way is being removed and you can see yourself where you want to be.

CHANT:
Something blocks my way ahead,
the path of my desire.
Let this stone, like beams of sun
melt barriers like fire.
No more delay gets in my way,
No obstacles resist.
For good off all, I will succeed,
my plan for change persists.
The goal I seek let now fulfill,
The outcome shall be as I will.

Combine this with candle magic if you'd like by burning a candle on your altar while you charge your stone(s) or jewelry. Use a white, yellow, or gold candle.

VARIATION:

For a more "dissolving" method, use azurite, which is associated with the element of Water. Carry a small stone with you or charge a piece of jewelry that contains azurite.

CHANT:

Something blocks my way ahead,
the path I seek to follow.
Let barriers erode away,
Washed by waves of water.
No more delay gets in my way,
No obstacles resist.
For good of all, I will succeed,
my plan for change persists.
The goal I seek let now fulfill,
The outcome shall be as I will.

Shield Spell

This spell calls for a pyrite "sun" which is a special formation of pyrite that looks like a flattened disc. These are sometimes sold as "pyrite dollars" or "marcasite dollars." Marcasite and pyrite are polymorphs (like diamond and graphite, which are both carbon). Pyrite and marcasite have the same chemical composition but have different structure and crystal shape. Marcasite is commonly used in jewelry.

The reason for this particular formation is not certain, but you should be able to find one at a gem and mineral shop. So far, the only known locality for these formations is the coal mines of Illinois. I happen to have two of these in my collection—I "lost" one so I bought another. Of course, after I bought the new one I found my first one. I guess the universe thought I needed two! The two I have are somewhat different in appearance and now I'm glad I have two different specimens.

We know pyrite as "fool's gold," and the name "pyrite" comes from the Greek *pyros*, meaning fire. Chipping at a piece of pyrite with another stone produces sparks; it is believed that Stone Age people used this method to make fire. Some sources say this stone should never be placed in water. Use your best judgment. Due to pyrite's association with the Fire element, sunlight is the best method for charging this particular stone.

Perform this spell during a waxing to full moon with the moon in Aries, if possible. Begin by charging your pyrite "sun" in full sunlight during a full moon phase. If you wish, place it on a bed of clear quartz crystal or on a bed of sea salt. Sometimes these specimens are sold with a tiny stand so they can be displayed like a decorative plate. You may use this stand if you choose. Visualize the stone absorbing the sun's rays and holding that powerful energy.

CHANT:
Pyrite Sun, catch this light,
hold this force both day and night.

Once you feel your stone has been sufficiently charged, proceed with the spell.

Hold the stone in your projective hand. Visualize it as an actual shield that would be used in battle. Imagine whatever you fear being repelled simply by the presence of this shield. Nothing can pierce it; it repels all negativity and is as blinding for enemies to look upon as a full blast of sunlight.

CHANT:

May this stone serve as a shield
adding to the strength I wield.
Hard as iron, bright as sun,
ill intent now be undone.

Carry the stone with you, or place the stone on a red cloth on your altar or other special place. While talismans and amulets are typically carried or worn, this spell will be just as effective if you keep the shield on your altar. If you choose this method, you can visualize the "shield" surrounding you no matter where you are. Obviously this is not a magic shield that will deflect blows (but how cool would that be); rather, the effect causes you to increase your awareness and focus.

Pyrite "Dollar" Spell

This spell uses the same pyrite formation as the Shield spell. The pyrite disc is sometimes called a "sun" or a "dollar." In this case, we will use the stone to represent wealth and combine this with a pyrite nugget you can carry.

YOU WILL ALSO NEED:

- a dollar bill

- a clear glass jar

- a green votive or tealight candle

- a piece of green or white fabric with a ribbon to tie it
  (or a green or white drawstring bag)

Charge your pyrite disc (and nugget) as directed in the Shield spell. In the jar, place a green candle charged for prosperity and put the small pyrite nugget in the jar next to the candle. Place the dollar bill on top of your pyrite disc, and set the jar on top of the bill. Visualize a connection between the stones and the candle—the pyrite "dollar" and candle adding rich, golden energy to the nugget. Light the candle and chant:

End of rainbow, pot of gold,
legends of a treasure told;
may your sparkle bring to me
wisdom and prosperity.

When the candle burns out and the wax cools, pick out the nugget of pyrite. Wrap the dollar bill around it and tie these into a bundle with the fabric and ribbon. Carry this talisman with you. Keep the pyrite "dollar" on your altar.

Making Your Own Magical Jewelry

If you can string beads on a wire, you can make your own jewelry—it can be that simple. A coven sister of mine taught me the basic technique and I've made dozens of necklaces, bracelets, and even earrings. In fact, she taught our entire coven so we could make jewelry together. If you want to learn jewelry-making techniques, find an instruction book or video to get started, or take a class at a craft store. In addition, like any handmade craft, you can easily make the act of jewelry-making into a ritual. Having your group learn together can be a wonderful bonding experience.

You can speak a specific word or phrase as you add each bead, then dedicate the finished piece for your purpose. You can also designate certain pieces of jewelry for special rituals and celebrations, such as moonstone for full moon rituals and smoky quartz or jet for the dark moon.

When shopping for jewelry and supplies, beware of cheap imitation stones and plastics. While inexpensive plastic beads can be good fashion pieces for casual wear, they do not make good magical jewelry. You may be wondering about glass beads. They're pretty, made of natural material, and come in every color you can imagine. There's nothing wrong with having a magical piece made of glass, depending on your purpose. Glass can be infused with personal power just like any craft. It's also nice to string glass beads together with real stone; this is what I recommend if you plan to use glass for magical jewelry. And don't forget about natural items like wood, pearls, and shells. Know your sources and never buy a piece that's endangered or illegally harvested. Wood and shell beads are usually inexpensive and easy to find.

Once you acquire some simple jewelry, making tools, you may be able to make simple repairs to broken pieces or take apart old pieces to make new ones. Speaking of broken jewelry, I once had a particular ring charged for magical purpose but, after just over a year of wearing it, the stone fell out. Luckily, I found the stone, so the ring could be repaired, but then I realized the need I had charged it for had been resolved. I set the ring aside (since having it repaired was going to cost more than I paid for the ring—it was an antique) and I started wearing a different ring on that finger—it turns out that this new ring I began wearing had a purpose. It was a stone associated with my astrological sign and after further research, I discovered that it indeed pertained to a personal issue I was dealing with. It's funny how these things turn out. So, pay attention to little signs, investigate stones that seem to "find" you, and you may end up addressing something in your life that needs attention.

Coven Jewelry

If you're a member of a group, circle, or coven, it's nice to have matching pieces of jewelry to wear for gatherings. If you purchase pendants, each person can personalize his or her piece by whatever chain or beads is desired. As a group, you can dedicate your pieces together during a ritual—it can be a powerful moment, and you'll have your piece of jewelry to feel that bond even when you're not together. You could also create personalized strings of beads that perhaps each contain some of the same stones. Or you could all learn to make jewelry together like we did!

Our coven has matching sterling silver pendants with a special symbol that holds meaning for us. However, each of us wears the symbol in her own way—I leave mine loose so I can change the chain; one of the other ladies has strung hers on beads made from one of her personal power stones. We dedicated our pieces in a group ritual using water from a sacred spring. Here's a chant you can use to dedicate group ritual jewelry (of course, you are encouraged to personalize this or write your own).

Put all the pieces together on the altar and chant:

By this symbol we are bound,
joined by friendship we have found.
Sisters/Companions in the craft unite
Near or far and day or night.
May these symbols keep us strong,
To each other we belong.

Each individual holds his/her piece and everyone chants:

Let these pieces serve and show
The sisterhood (companionship) in which we grow.
Dedicate them all as one,
As we will, so it be done.

Put on the jewelry.

Cleansing Secondhand Jewelry

Some of the most interesting and unique pieces of gemstone jewelry can be found in secondhand and antique shops. You can find good deals at garage sales, as well as online.

I once found a gorgeous pair of natural quartz point earrings in a secondhand shop in Seattle. I have pendants of amethyst and malachite, rings of onyx, garnet, and tiger eye, all purchased via online auctions, all previously owned. In one antique shop I bought an amazing amber ring set in sterling silver. You can find some great deals on gently used jewelry, so don't pass them up.

Of course, you may be concerned about the energy the object holds from its previous owner. This spell is intended to remove any lingering, unwanted baggage.

Cleansing Ritual

Using a mortar and pestle, grind dried rosemary with a tablespoon of sea salt or a few grains of frankincense. Let the item rest on the mixture for 24 hours. Visualize the piece being purified and belonging to you. Or, you can use a cleansing elixir (chapter four).

CHANT:
Stone(s) not new, but new to me,
I now claim ownership of thee.
Clear of former energy—
For good of all, so mote it be.

Parting with a Piece of Magical Jewelry

So, what do you do if a piece of jewelry you own comes to have negativity associated with it? When a relationship breaks up, people often have mixed emotions about the symbolic jewelry that bound them together. This is true for marriages, engagements, friendships, and even covens. Some people simply can't bring themselves to part with a memory. They tuck away the item in a box, put the box in a drawer, and move on. For some people that's fine, especially if there are no hard feelings left in the relationship. But what if there are lingering feelings of negativity? What if you can't stand to even have the item in your home?

I know someone who went through a situation like this. Not only were there bad memories of betrayal associated with a piece of jewelry, she was also concerned that the piece was a link that kept her tied to this person; she wanted to sever the relationship completely and move on. First, she put the item in a bed of salt while she decided how to handle it. She went over various solutions, such as giving it away, burying it, or throwing it in the garbage. In the end, she cleansed the piece well and donated it to a store so it could be sold to someone else. She felt that this benefitted everyone and didn't do any harm to the memory of her failed relationship. Once she was rid of that physical reminder, the healing began.

If you feel you must part with a piece of jewelry, give it some time. Let the piece rest out of sight for a while. You may have more options than you realize. You can have metals melted down and stones reset. I know a married couple who each saved their rings from previous relationships and as a symbol of their new love, had the rings melted down together. New rings were made from the gold, and the diamonds were set in them. They each held on to these rings for many years before making this decision, and the newly created rings were not their wedding rings, only for general wear. Nevertheless, it was a deeply symbolic way to recycle the materials.

A special piece could become a family heirloom, passed along from person to person. A ring from a relationship that didn't work out could be given to a relative for a new relationship, though it's important to cleanse it first.

There's nothing wrong with keeping a piece of jewelry if you have good memories associated with it. Just clean and cleanse it before storing it away. This will help remove negativity—and it's a symbolic clearing of the old to make way for the new. If you have very strong emotions, but still don't want to permanently give up the piece, ask a friend to store it for you or put it in a safe-deposit box.

Sometimes, for whatever reason, we feel that a piece used in a spell can't be cleansed enough, and we would rather be rid of it. A ritual parting for a broken or lost piece that still contains magical energy can offer a sense of closure.

Parting Ritual

During a waning moon phase, place the item on a bed of sea salt crystals. Visualize the item being neutralized and purified.

CHANT:

Symbol of what used to be,
Symbol I no longer need,
A peaceful resolution found,
For good of all, no longer bound.

Keep the object on the salt until the new moon. Then decide how to dispose of it. It can be as easy as placing it in a box and stow it away in a drawer if you're comfortable with that. Another idea is to have the piece taken apart and made into something new (if possible). Ask yourself if destroying the piece is really necessary. If it is, find a safe way to discard it.

If the piece has been lost and you seek a symbolic parting, place a drawing or photo of it upon the salt and follow the same directions. When the ritual is complete, destroy the photo or drawing.

To dispose of a bundle, simply disassemble it and recycle the pieces. Cleanse any stones you plan to use again; bury herbs. Wash the ribbons and cloth, burn them, or throw them away. Sometimes candle wax can be recycled if you make candles; otherwise, throw it away.

– THREE –

CRYSTAL SPELLS FOR THE HOME AND GARDEN

Introduction

It's probably no surprise that I have stones in every room of my house *and* in the yard. Giant geodes rest on bookcases in my living room; candle holders made of alabaster and quartz sit on tables and shelves; clusters (seen and unseen) are tucked in various places in the bedroom, bathroom, and kitchen. I also have a couple of those decorative fountains, the ones that promote the relaxing sound of water dripping over rocks—of course, I added some of my own stones and crystal points. If I look out my patio door, I can see a large chunk of quartz glittering on a plant stand; a small shimmering geode is half-buried in the soil of a planter box. Other tiny points are hidden in the vegetable garden and in containers. Just like each room of the house, nearly every flower bed in my yard has some type of stone to adorn it. Some have a magical purpose, others are for decoration.

The spells in this chapter are for the placement of stones in specific rooms of the house or in the yard, intended to enhance the energy. The stone or stones should be set in place with specific intent and visualization. This makes them more than merely decorative—they have purpose, even if you're the only one who knows it.

The Home: Room by Room

Clusters are always a good choice for the home, as they promote a sense of community and harmony among groups—perfect for family units. Any clear quartz cluster is appropriate for all home and garden use. That being said, there are certain qualities we can promote in each specific room. Let's explore the house and make some magic!

Kitchen and Dining Room

Have you ever noticed that people at parties tend to gather in the kitchen, even if there's another spacious room? The kitchen is the "hearth" space, the center of the home in many ways, even if families don't gather together for regular meals every day. Here are some good stone choices for kitchen crystal magic:

- **Agates** are grounding, promote general good health and longevity, and generate a calming environment.

- **Amazonite** and **galena** can be used for harmony.

- **Chrysocolla** purifies home environments in general, and promotes love, communication, and understanding; **fossils** are also good stabilizers for all environments.

- **Jasper** promotes a nurturing atmosphere.

Find a place to put your stone or stones—it's up to you if you want them to be seen or not. You can stash them in a cabinet, if you'd like. Incorporate them into a table centerpiece, or simply place them on a shelf or window ledge. A pretty rock on a windowsill looks nice, especially accompanied with herbs or flowers. Additionally, if you have potted plants you can add stones to them—see the section on gardens in this chapter.

Select your stone or combination of stones, or a crystal cluster. Cleanse and charge or dedicate as desired. Here's a chant to use as you place your stone(s), visualizing your specific goal(s):

> *With the placement of this/these stone(s)*
> *nurture now our hearth and home.*
> *Energize with festive mood*
> *where we nourish with good food.*
> *Keep us open, hearts and minds,*
> *let love guide us; words be kind.*

Bathroom

Bathrooms are a room of escape for some people—a private place for relaxing with a nice hot bath or shower, sometimes a place for pampering, a facial, manicure, or other aspects of a beauty regimen. These rooms can be elegant spa-like retreats, complete with candles and even plants, or tiny rooms that are purely functional with no decorative touches of any kind. Sometimes we're there just for a quick visit or taking care of personal hygiene, but the bathroom should not be overlooked as a place for magic. Even if you don't think you spend a lot of time in this room, it's a very personal (and necessary) place. A sense of tranquility should be found there; that may be difficult if you're sharing one bathroom with several people. If that's the case, this room can use all the tranquility it can get! Plus, it's often a place we end up in when we aren't feeling well physically, so some nurturing and healing properties are good qualities to encourage.

If you want to keep things simple, a quartz cluster works well. You could also simply place a stone on a shelf, or on the edge of the sink or tub. You can even keep one in the shower. Here are some other good choices:

- **Green fluorite** clears and creates a "fresh" feeling.

- **Peridot** is a good healing stone that regulates cycles.

- **Galena** promotes harmony, grounding, and centering.

- **Jasper** is used for nurturing, healing, and beauty.

Place stones as desired and use this chant:

Calm, serene, this room shall be
a peaceful place for what we need.
Refresh, renew, and keep us well,
stress and strain this stone dispel.

Also, don't overlook the use of bath salts. Remember: salt is a mineral! Making your own bath salts charged with magical energy can be a powerful spell. You can also charge bath salts you have purchased.

Here's a recipe for a small batch of general bath salts: Start with 2 cups of sea salt, and add several drops of your favorite essential oil. Add dried herbs or flowers if you like. Mix well and store in a jar with a tight lid. Charge your salt for whatever magical intent you need. Toss a handful of the salt beneath warm running water and visualize your intent; combine your bath with crystal or candle magic—or both.

Bedroom

Another room of retreat, the bedroom should be the epitome of relaxation—a place for rest, sleep, dreaming, sometimes healing, and, of course, love. It is a room that should be quiet and serene, the place we close our day and begin anew.

GOOD STONE CHOICES FOR THE BEDROOM ARE:

- **Rose quartz**—promotes universal love, emotions, forgiveness

- **Unakite**—like rose quartz, but with a more grounding quality

- **Moonstone**—calming, intuition

- **Amethyst**—aids sleep, peaceful, spiritual

- **Garnet**—to remember dreams, also for love and patience

- **Lepidolite**—dispels nightmares, reduces stress and anxiety, creates a calming environment

- **Mica**—aids sleep

- **Milky quartz**—stabilizes dreams

- **Rhondonite**—love, calming

- **Rhodochrosite**—love, emotional balance, health

Use the stone or stones of your choice, visualize your intent, and chant:

Calm and gentle energy,
A loving, peaceful place to be:
On this room I now bestow
Soothing magic from these stones/this stone.

State your purpose.

Office or Study

Whether our workspace is at home or at an outside location (or a combination of both), we need to focus but we also want the ability to be calm under stress. Here are some good stones for a variety of work environments or the home study area:

- **Hematite**—manual dexterity, a stone of the mind

- **Agate**—grounding, personal development

- **Amazonite**—helps eliminate aggravation

- **Aragonite**—fosters patience, helps one accept responsibilities

- **Citrine**—the merchant's stone, education, business, mental clarity, communication

- **Fluorite**—all colors: discernment and aptitude

- **Howlite**—aids and calms communication, encourages subtlety and tact

- **Jet**—protects business and finance

- **Lodestone**—motivation and purpose

- **Pyrite**—shields from negative energy, enhances memory and understanding

- **Petrified wood**—helps relieve work-related stress

- **Rutilated quartz**—stimulates brain function, stimulates inspiration

- **Tourmalinated quartz**—creates a "solving" atmosphere

- **Sodalite**—logic and objectivity

- **Sulfur**—gently melts barriers toward progress

- **Tiger eye**—focus and concentration, prosperity, helps manifest ideas into reality

- **Vanadinite**—facilitates mental processes, bridges thought and intelligence

Visualize your specific need and chant:

May it now be known,
The purpose of this stone/these stones,
I place with pure intent,
to let it represent/them represent
the qualities I seek—
I will it as I speak:

State your purpose.

Den/Family Room/Living Room

For these social places in the home where people gather for fun and entertainment, clusters of clear quartz are especially useful. If you place them in a visible location, they also make good conversation pieces. This room is an excellent place to display stone candle-holders, if you have them. Of course, you can also select a specific stone for a particular need you may have. Visualize your desired outcome and chant:

Family and friends,
a place to entertain,
a place for joy and peace—
Let this stone maintain.

Balancing Your Home: The Center and the Four Corners

The purpose of this spell is to identify the "center" of your home and the four corners, in order to bring balance. If you have a floor plan of your dwelling, that would be ideal; if not, sketch one yourself. Using a compass, find north and label each direction on your sketched diagram or floor plan.

If you have a multi-level home, decide which floor "feels" like the center of the dwelling. If you have a basement and two floors, perhaps use the main floor. Some people may prefer to use the basement. Or, there may be an area on the upper level that seems "right" for the center. The choice is yours.

To keep the energy in your home stable, you can place a large quartz cluster at or near the center (in this case, size does matter—clusters have more energy than a single point). If this area is a room, you may be able to simply use a decorative method for your stone(s). If this space is a closet, you can tuck a stone or stones on a shelf or in a box. Try to get as close to the center as you can. Next, try to place similar stones at each of the four directions. Again, do your best to work with the space that is available. For the corners, you may use single points. Aim the point toward the center of your home.

The idea of "Center and Four Corners" is intended to bring balance and harmony to your home's energy. After you place the stones, visualize a line of energy connecting each stone, like a web or network of cables, a connection between all of them, like beams of light or energy. Start from the center, move out to each corner and back again, and link the corners to each other.

Note: the four corners for balance don't necessarily have to be the perfect four directions. Your house may be a perfect square, but not correspond exactly with north, south, east, and west. That's fine—use the four corners for balance to link with the center stone. After all the stones are in place, chant:

Crystal cluster mark this center,
Permit no ill intent to enter.
Quarter crystals marking four,
Guard each room, window, and door.
Energy ceiling to floor,
Every space, closet and drawer.
Link with center, four makes five,
Balanced now, all here will thrive.

VARIATIONS:

- You can link this with one of the protection wards for outside the home.

- Feel free to adapt this for whatever living arrangements you have, or use this for a single room, if you're in a dorm room, for example.

- In addition, use a pendulum to dowse your floor plan to locate specific areas that need balance. You can also do this for each individual room.

Outside the Home: Protection and Boundaries

Unfortunately, we usually can't choose our neighbors. In any instance when you're concerned about property boundaries (for privacy or other reasons) a fence is the logical choice, if possible. If you have a fence, you can enforce it with crystal magic. If having a fence is not an option, bury stones in the ground to serve as a metaphysical boundary. The strategic planting of trees and shrubs is also useful for creating a border. Plants that climb trellises are excellent choices and can work in an apartment as well. Use potted plants on balconies and rooftops, or try window boxes. You can even put a trellis inside a planter box and grow a vine on it, creating a flowering wall. Add stones to the planter boxes. As you place your stones, use the appropriate chant for your need.

To Protect Property Lines

For this spell you will need three or four anchor stones to place outside. You can put one at each corner of your property or just scatter them, one in the front yard or on the porch, the others on the side or in the back.

Set the anchor stones in plain view as ornaments or conceal them beneath bushes or in flower beds. You can also use existing items in the landscape to help anchor your ward if you'd like, especially large trees, fences, or other landmarks. Use this ward for protection and to keep out unwanted energy and trespassers. Visualize these stones as anchors for a protective net or screen with the stones holding it in place. Make a clockwise path around your home and with the placement of each stone, say:

Keep all negativity at bay,
Keep all danger far away
Each stone set in place—
A ward protects this space.

When you have set all the stones, complete the spell by visualizing energy linking the stones together; this forms a bond that keeps out unwanted energy and entities.

WARD FOR BOUNDARIES:

Here's a simpler version: place any type of stones along your property lines, and visualize the stones creating an invisible boundary.

Here I mark a border line, this boundary can't be crossed
by anyone who means me harm—if so, they pay the cost.

FOR PEACE AND PRIVACY:

Similar to the Ward for Boundaries, use this spell to increase privacy. Place stones either along property lines or in gardens, containers, et cetera.

> *Within these bounds my privacy, protected and preserved;*
> *Let no disturbance enter here, my peacefulness deserved.*

To Protect Entryways

You can even attach quartz points to wreaths on your door or hang them in windows. Combine them for a quick protection spell. Visualize your need and use this chant:

> *Crystal in my window,*
> *Crystal at my door,*
> *Crystal guard this dwelling—*
> *Safe for evermore.*

GENERAL HOME PROTECTION:

Here's an additional spell you can use for protection. Visualize, place the stones, and chant:

> *With intent I place this stone/these stones,*
> *May it/they safely guard my home.*
> *Keep the balance and the peace,*
> *All disruptions now will cease.*

Stone Spells for the Garden

I must give a certain amount of credit to my mother and grandmother for my love of stones. I grew up appreciating the rock gardens they each constructed in their yards—rings of stone around roses and glass gazing balls on pedestals, stone walls shimmering with bits of crystal, and rocks worn by water into interesting shapes. I remember searching creek beds with them for these water-worn stones (Grandma always said that a stone with a hole worn through would bring good luck). Now, a flower garden doesn't seem complete to me without some kind of decorative stone.

You can completely hide the stones if you'd like, but leaving them out adds a decorative element to the garden. Or you can bury them partially, in rock garden style. The key to creating a natural-looking rock garden is to bury the stones in the soil so only part of them peek above the surface, giving the appearance that the stones have always been part of the landscape. This can be done for a small container up to the largest backyard boulders you can imagine. Then, simply plant around the stones. Use ground covers, grasses, annuals and perennials, herbs, trees and shrubs, or even vegetables. You can weave a spell into any type of rock garden. No matter how big or small your space, you can create an enchanting rock garden.

Most nurseries sell garden stones, many types and sizes, but I usually prefer to find my own. Choose the method that works best for you. A simple Internet search will generate hundreds of photos to inspire your project. Rock gardening can be simple and small or a very expensive entire yard make-over. You can transform an existing garden space, or simply add stones to flowers beds and vegetable gardens. Raised beds, containers, hanging baskets, window and fence boxes, whether they contain herbs, vegetables, flowers, or foliage plants are all appropriate places for crystal magic.

You can add stones to other outdoor features such as water gardens, fountains, fire rings—anything you can think of. I have a large fountain on my patio that has a place on top for stones, much like the indoor relaxation fountain, the intent being that the water running over them adds to the pleasant sound. Some tumbled stones were included when the fountain was purchased but, of course, I added some of my own into the assortment—beautifully banded agate that looks even lovelier when wet, and granite. This is a great way to use crystal magic outside, and also include the Water element (see Fountain Spell at the end of this chapter).

Here are some spells for specific types of gardens. Since there are endless types of garden combinations, choose your stones from the list and find an appropriate chant for your need or simply place a stone near the plant for a harmonious relationship.

Complementary Combinations for the Garden

These are mainly based on planetary correspondences.

- **Amber:** Place near sap-filled trees to strengthen them.

- **Amethyst:** honeysuckle, linden, maple, sage

- **Apache tear, Hematite, Onyx, Serpentine, Obsidian:** amaranth, asphodel, beech, beet, cypress, elm, hemp, ivy, lady's slipper, morning glory, mullein, pansy, poplar, wolf's bane, yew

- **Aventurine:** almond, aspen, bean, Brazil nut, caraway, celery, clover, dill, fennel, fern, lavender, lemongrass, lily of the valley, marjoram, May apple, mint, mulberry, parsley, pecan, peppermint

- **Bloodstone, Pyrite:** basil, broom, cactus, carrot, chili pepper, coriander, garlic, ginger, hawthorn, holly, hops, horseradish, leek, mustard, nettle, onion, pennyroyal, pepper, peppermint, pine, radish, shallot, snapdragon, thistle, wormwood, yucca

- **Citrine, Carnelian:** cedar, chamomile, marigold, oak, orange, rosemary, St. John's Wort, rowan, rue, sunflower, walnut, witch hazel

- **Jade, Sodalite:** African violet, apple, apricot, aster, avocado, bachelor's buttons, banana, birch, blackberry, bleeding heart, catnip, cherry, columbine, crocus, daffodil, daisy, elder, foxglove, geranium, goldenrod, hibiscus, hyacinth, iris, lilac, mugwort, orchid, passion flower, pea, peach, pear, persimmon, plum, raspberry, rhubarb, rose, spearmint, strawberry, sweetpea, thyme, tomato, tulip, valerian, vervain, violet, wheat, willow

- **Jet:** Use near shade-loving plants to strengthen them.

- **Lapis lazuli:** Use for general soil fertility.

- **Moonstone:** aloe, coconut, cucumber, eucalyptus, grape, gardenia, jasmine, lettuce, lemon, lily, lotus, poppy, potato, willow

- **Turquoise:** Place near plants that are recovering from pest attack or disease.

- **Clear quartz** is appropriate for all plants to encourage general good health and enhance growth.

VEGETABLE GARDENS:

Bury a stone in your garden, in one corner, or every corner. As you place each stone, visualize your need and chant:

Nourish us with healthy food
This I ask for highest good.

HERB GARDENS:

Use this chant as you place each stone:

Herbs for magic, herbs for spice,
with this stone, my goal precise.
Grow and flourish, leaf and flower,
Cultivate your special power.

ORCHARDS AND FRUIT/BERRY VINES:

Visualize a bountiful harvest and chant:

Fruit for sharing, fruit to eat,
with this stone, the yield be sweet.

SEEDS/SEEDLINGS:

Visualize the seedlings growing as you chant:

Take root, grow strong,
new plants, live long.

OTHER PLANTS:

Grow and bloom, flourish bright,
with this stone, banish blight.
Keep disease and pests away,
healthy plants in vast array.

FAIRY GARDENS:

It has been my experience that the Fae enjoy having pretty, spar-
kling stones in the garden. It doesn't have to be only clear quartz; you
can incorporate any rocks you find that have a lovely appearance. Holey

stones and geodes are nice choices as well. After placing the stones, visualize and chant:

Welcome, Fae, to this place
filled with peace; bring your grace.

Garden Protection Spell

In addition to whatever methods you use to keep pests out of the garden, a little magic can't hurt. I try to keep a harmonious yard a habitat for wildlife, but sometimes even the friendly squirrels and rabbit chew on some plants. Provide food for them, and water. This may help deter them. Sprinkling crushed red pepper around your plants may deter them, or consider providing some special plants as food just for wildlife.

For this spell, place a clear quartz point in each corner of the garden. Chant as you place each stone:

Creatures though I welcome thee,
Kindly let my garden be.
Please don't harm my plants or home
I ask this while I place this stone.

To avoid losing small crystals in the garden or in large flower beds, place them next to a large rock so you can locate them—sometimes small stones become buried after a strong rain. Another option is to use specimens you don't mind parting with. Often you can purchase low-quality pieces from rock shops or jewelry suppliers.

Fountain Spell

Because I'm so fond of fountains, both indoors and out, I like to use them in spells to incorporate all the elements. Near a fountain of running water and stones, light a candle. In this way, you're utilizing Earth, Air, Fire, and Water. Some fountains are even made with built-in candle-holders. Select stones based on your need and charge them. Light the candle, visualize, and chant while holding the stone(s):

> *Earth and Water, Air and Fire*
> *Grant the wish that I desire.*
> *For good of all and harm to none,*
> *As I will it shall be done.*

State your goal; place the stone(s) in the fountain.

– FOUR –

CRYSTAL ELIXIRS
AND ESSENCES

Introduction

If there is a true elixir of life, it is water. Not only essential for life, it is perhaps where life began. Combine water with crystals to make an elixir, and you have a potent metaphysical potion.

It is believed by some that the thoughts we project and the words we say can have an effect on the crystals that form from water. Dr. Masaru Emoto seeks to prove this in his book *The Hidden Messages in Water*. In magical practice, we believe that our intent does have power. If we can project this into crystals and even more easily into water, crystal elixirs can be a powerful catalyst for magic. Our thoughts affect our body. We are what we think. When you make an elixir to drink or otherwise, think of it as a potion or tonic for change, a transmitter of messages, a way to manifest your intent, emotions, and thoughts.

Elixirs and gem essences are made by soaking a stone in water, with the metaphysical intent of infusing the water with that crystal's energy. There is a difference between elixirs and essences, and most are not intended to be consumed—they are intended mainly for spells and rituals. I can't stress this enough: **The elixirs and essences (with the exception of the drinkable clear quartz elixir) in this book are *not* intended to be ingested.** Some minerals are toxic, and some you think are safe may actually contain traces of toxic minerals. The only elixir I would ever consider drinking is clear quartz, and that would only be a sip or two. **Be aware that some sources say that no stone is really safe for this purpose.** If you want to drink the water, I recommend the "dry" method of making an elixir, a practice we will explore in this chapter. Using that method, you can use any stone you'd like, as long as it doesn't come into contact with the water at any time. Always use care handling any stone you are unsure of, especially any metallic stone or those that are blue or green in color (these often contain copper).

In medieval Europe, stone elixirs were used to create amulets and talismans. It was believed that the stone should be placed in a vessel made of gold or silver and then filled with wine. This mixture was left in moonlight for three days. The wine could then be consumed, and the stone was ready (charged) to be used for creating an amulet or talisman. You can try this method to charge a stone but, again, I don't recommend drinking the liquid. You can pour it onto the ground as an offering.

Elixirs and Essences: The Difference

The main difference between these stone and water "infusions" is as follows:

- Elixir: A stone left in water for a period of time.

- Essence: A stone left in water for a period of time intended for long-term storage—a preservative is added, such as vodka or vinegar, since essences often contain herbs and essential oils.

- **"Dry" Elixir:** The stone is not actually immersed in the water so you can take advantage of the stone's energy in a subtle way. This is also called the indirect method.

The reason it's a good idea to add a preservative when using herbs is that the plant materials break down and can "rot" in the water. If you want to avoid using a preservative but still want to use herbs in your elixirs, create an herbal infusion (like making tea) before you add the stone and charge it. Brewing and straining will create an infusion that can be stored longer.

Basic Elixir (Not for consumption)

1. Choose a stone and charge it for your purpose.

2. Select your water and container. I recommend making a crystal elixir from water you have gathered from a spring or other natural source. You can also use rainwater or melted snow. You may wish to use a decorative bottle with a cork or a jar with a screw-top lid.

3. Decide on a method: sunlight or moonlight, or both. See the Suggestions section for a variety of ideas and chants.

4. Use whatever visualization technique you feel is appropriate. You can imagine the light seeping through, penetrating the crystal (charged with your intent) and then transferring that energy to the water. If you'd like, you can arrange clear quartz points around the container, points facing inward. Or surround the vessel with a ring of stones of your choice, depending on the elixir's intended purpose or stones that correspond to the sun and moon.

5. Storage: If you don't add herbs or oils, pour the water into the storage container you have selected (unless you created it in that container). You may leave the stone in the container (make sure it's not a water-soluble stone). A simple stone in water elixir can be stored for a long time, but it can go magically "stale." This water is best used for cleansing stones or other consecration purposes. You may let this sit on your altar if you'd like.

6. When you're done with the stone, cleanse it and recharge it in sunlight or moonlight if you like. Try to avoid making another elixir with this stone for a few months—let it rest.

Basic Essence (Not for consumption)

These are often blended with herbs and oils and are intended for long-term storage.

1. Follow the procedure for an elixir by adding a stone to water in a glass container.

2. Allow the mixture to sit in sunlight or moonlight for at least 6 hours. In a separate glass container that seals well, pour in half vodka or vinegar and half of your crystal infusion.

3. Remove the stone (or leave it in, if you prefer).

4. Add herbs or herbal infusions, oils, etc., as desired. You can add herbs and oils before allowing the mixture to sit in sunlight or moonlight but heat will diminish the scent of the essential oils.

5. You can use this mixture to blend with other essences and elixirs.

Here's a chant to use for an essence:

Infuse and store this crystal's power,
Growing purer by the hour.
Potent essence, stone and water,
Make my magic all the stronger.

Indirect, or "Dry," Elixir

This method seeks to capture the energy of the stone without submerging it in water. This is an excellent choice for stones that are water soluble or metallic stones that are toxic. Place the stone inside a glass container *without water*, and cover it with a secure lid—a jar works well for this. Then, place the dry container inside another glass container and add water to the outer container. If you use an inner container that seals tightly, you can completely submerge this in water. Otherwise, just add water that halfway covers the inner container. Place the containers in sun or moonlight. If you start with water that is safe to drink you can consume this elixir—*but be sure the water never comes into contact with the stone.* And, of course, make sure the containers are clean inside and out. When placing an elixir in sunlight or moonlight outside, you may wish to cover your container(s) with plastic wrap so the wind doesn't blow in any foreign objects (or bugs!). You could also cover the container with a clear glass plate. Also be sure to wash your hands after handling any metallic stone.

Elixir and Essence Suggestions

- You *can* add herbs and essential oils to an elixir. A mixture of water, a few drops of oil, some herbs, and a crystal can be combined to make a nice room-cleansing mist or bath oil. Remember to use this mixture within a few days, especially if you add herbs to the water. You can store this elixir longer if you make an infusion of the herbs rather than actually adding herbs to the water.

- Some of the spells in this book call for a particular type of elixir; it's useful to keep these on hand. You may wish to create a fresh batch during each full moon.

- Store your elixir or essence in a dark-colored glass jar or bottle with a tight lid. You can accumulate these by simply saving containers you buy other products in, such as vinegar or salad oils, even spices.

- Another way to use elixirs is to make gem oils for massage— first, make the carrier oil base, then let your stone sit in the oil for a few hours. Use the oil for bath or massage. Be sure to follow aromatherapy guidelines for safety. Oils you purchase should have information on the label.

- To create a dark moon elixir, use a piece of obsidian and leave the water outside during a new moon. This elixir would be suitable for a mist to dispel negativity or to cleanse an object. You could also add this to water for a purification bath.

- You can collect morning dew from plants using an eyedropper and add this to an elixir. Or use melted snow, rainwater, or water collected from a special place. Remember—only drink water that is safe. When in doubt, don't drink it!

- Soak a cloth in elixir or essence and rest it on parts of the body.

Sun Elixir

Use this elixir for any spell involving solar energy, projective energy, success, strength, or protection. Let it set in sunlight as long as you like, but remove it before nightfall. Try to make this during a waxing to full moon phase, even though you're making "sun" elixir. A piece of amber is an excellent stone to use. Visualize the light entering the stone, penetrating, and then passing into the water, infusing it, drawing the minerals from the stone into the liquid, their molecules making a metaphysical connection.

> CHANT:
>
> *By light of sun, this water be*
> *charged with crystal energy.*
> *Sunlight warm, shining through*
> *Water clear, fresh and new.*

Moon Elixir

Use this elixir for any spell involving lunar energy, receptive energy, emotions, love, or intuition. Make this elixir during the full moon. Let this set in moonlight as long as you like, but remove it before sunrise. Moonstone would be a good choice for this elixir.

> CHANT:
>
> *By light of moon, this water be*
> *charged with crystal energy.*
> *Moonlight soft, silver glow*
> *Water clear, flow and grow.*

Cleansing and Protection Elixir

This elixir combines salt, frankincense resin, rosemary, lemon, and cedar essential oil to dispel negative energy and provide protection. First, boil water as you would for tea. Pour the water into a glass bowl and add the rosemary (fresh or dried). You can make a cheesecloth bundle, use a teabag, or leave the herbs loose. Cut the end of a lemon and squeeze the juice into the bowl; then toss the end piece in as well. Add 3 grains of sea salt and 1 small piece of frankincense resin while the water is still warm. Let this mixture steep to create an infusion. When the water cools, strain the mixture into a spray bottle. Add a clear quartz point and 3 drops of cedar essential oil. Let the elixir sit in sunlight for a few hours or all day. Optional: for a sweeter scent, add a few drops of orange essential oil. Spray as desired, and use the mixture within a few months.

This elixir is a good choice for when you have to use any space that has recently been occupied by another (especially if you know there has been negativity.) It is excellent for dorm rooms, apartments, hotel rooms, offices, or even in used automobiles. After an argument, it can be used to "clear the air." You may also spray it outside the home and near entryways and windows. As you spray, visualize and chant:

> *Clear the air, clean it, too.*
> *Make this place, safe and new.*

Elixir to Dispel Negative Energy

An elixir similar to the Cleansing and Protection one can be created to clear disturbances from the astral plane. Begin with a dark moon elixir, created during a waning moon. Add 9 grains of sea salt, a few sprigs of dried rosemary, a drop of cedar oil, and 3 drops of frankincense essential oil (or one grain of frankincense resin). Transfer the mixture to a spray bottle and use where needed or place a drop of it on a stone and put the stone in a specific place where a disturbance is felt or suspected. A quartz cluster is the best choice, as the liquid can slide down into the crevasses and won't run off. Since this mixture contains herbs and is not strained, use it quickly or dispose of it.

CHANT:
Uninvited and unwanted
Let this source of ill be hunted.
Chased away with harm to none,
Leave this place, my will be done.

Home Blessing Elixir

Create this elixir during a waxing moon. Begin with 2 cups general quartz elixir or essence. If you didn't leave the stone in the container, add one now. Add 6 grains of sea salt and place the mixture in sunlight for 2 hours. Add 1 teaspoon fresh lemon juice. Transfer the mixture to a spray bottle. Use this to mist each room of a new dwelling or to freshen as needed. Visualize this as a spiritual cleansing and blessing for your home. Repeat annually or quarterly.

CHANT:
Bless this home, clean and clear,
Guard all those who enter here.
No ill will, with this charm,
Keep us safe from any harm.

Calming Elixir

Begin with a general crystal elixir. Blend this half and half with a fresh amethyst elixir. Bathe in it, apply to skin, or wet a cloth and rest it on your forehead. Visualize the cool, soothing color of amethyst. See those characteristics calming your mind. If you'd like, store this mixture in the refrigerator for an extra-cooling effect.

Chant these words over and over, like a mantra:

Calm and soothe, chill my mood.

Elixir for Passion

This elixir can be used to revive the physical aspect of a relationship. During a waxing moon phase, create an elixir using carnelian—place in sunlight for six hours. Visualize the mixture as being infused with whatever type of energy you desire for your specific situation. Use this water in a bath or to anoint your body, especially the sacral chakra. Or, for a more intense experience, you can add massage oil to the elixir and enjoy it with your partner. You can also create a "dry" sun elixir with carnelian and drink it. Perhaps add a few drops to some cocktails!

Chant these words over the mixture when you prepare it and before you use it:

Liquid passion, crystal potion,
Stimulate the body's motion.
By the power of the sun
For good of all, let it be done.

Full Moon Bath Tonic

First, create a basic elixir using moonstone. Optional: Add a few drops of morning dew gathered on Beltane or at midsummer. As you pour this elixir into the bath, visualize the radiance of the full moon infusing the water.

CHANT:
Liquid moonlight bring to me
beauty and tranquility.
Water give me gracefulness
as my body you caress.

Elixir for Beauty

Make an elixir using jasper and charge using your method of choice. There are many forms of jasper so select the variety that appeals to you. Jasper is a form of chalcedony (quartz), usually opaque, and is found in nearly every color, some with decorative spots and patterns. Add a small amount of this elixir to the water when you wash your face and visualize it as a youthful tonic, refreshing you and revealing your beauty at any age. Repeat this chant as you wash:

Years be gentle, time be kind,
Keep the beauty that is mine.
Wash away what worries me,
Leave a freshness all can see.

Drinkable Clear Quartz Elixir

1. Choose a clear quartz piece (point or tumbled) and be sure it's clean. To clean it, you can put the quartz in boiling water for a brief time, remove it with tongs, and allow it to cool. You can also wash the stone with mild dish soap as you would wash your dishes, and rinse it well.

2. You may charge the crystal for whatever purpose you like. Clear quartz is a good general energy and balancing stone. You can use it for any magical purpose by programming the stone with your intent.

3. Use drinking water, bottled or from the tap. You may use any amount—by the glass or a pitcher. Place the stone in the water.

4. You can place the container in sunlight or moonlight if you wish. Allow the crystal to sit in the water for up to twelve hours. Then, you can either remove the stone or keep it in the pitcher or glass—just be careful you don't swallow it!

5. Use this elixir immediately or keep it refrigerated for up to three days.

Salt Water Elixirs

Salt is one of the most popular minerals we use in our everyday lives. Magically, salt is traditionally used for cleansing, purification, and protection. Sea salt is evaporated sea water and is the preferred salt to use in magic. Depending on the stone(s) you're using, add the salt either before or after making the elixir. Obviously, the salt will dissolve better if you add it before allowing the water to sit for several hours; it's up to you. This type of elixir is a good choice for consecrating sacred space or tools, but be careful: too much salt can be harmful to some surfaces. Just use a pinch.

ADDITIONAL USES FOR ELIXIRS AND ESSENCES:

• add to bath for purification, healing, or any ritual bath— even wash your hair with it

• wash your face or anoint parts of your body

• cleanse stones, consecrate magical tools, or anoint objects

- float a candle on it

- add to a decorative fountain

- use it to water plants or use as an offering in garden magic

– FIVE –

SAND AND GLASS SPELLS

Sand Magic

Sand is essentially moveable rock, a collection of tiny crushed minerals and other organic substances. According to the International Sand Collector's Society: "Stones are primordial matter. Sand is matter ground by the infinity of time. It makes one mindful of eternity. Sand is matter which has been transformed and has almost become liquid and spiritual." Yes, there are sand collectors—a testament to the fascinating qualities of sand. Ground by time, sand is ancient and can be a powerful magical ingredient.

Look closely at sand; examine it with a magnifying glass. It's made up of tiny bits of ground stone and minerals. Like soil, sand is associated with the Earth element. Stone and crystal magic includes sand because it's made up of these tiny particles. You can combine sand and stones or simply use sand by itself in a spell.

Sand is fun to play with—what child, or even adult, can resist playing in the sand at the beach or in a sandbox? We like the way it feels under our feet and in our hands. We can mold it, shape it, and then crumble it and start over. Its fine grains are smooth and relaxing to touch.

Of course, sand has long been used in many types of art—it's a creative medium to work with. Colored sands can be layered in containers or used to create images such as the detailed mandalas of Tibetan Buddhists that are ritually destroyed after they are so painstakingly created. Zen gardens (Japanese rock gardens) use lines in sand to represent ripples on water, surrounded by the artful arrangement of plants and rocks. Beautiful sand castles and other sculptures have been made on beaches only to be washed away—such is the temporary nature of sand, reminding us that nothing lasts forever.

If we consider sand's many practical uses—it's an ingredient in concrete, in mortar to bind stones and bricks, and in making glass and computer chips—we know it's just one more way that stone is a vital part of our lives. Sand is often overlooked in magic, or reduced simply to a base material in a dish for burning incense or candles. And while it is an excellent choice for candle holders and incense burners, try to remember it can have magical significance.

You can buy sand at garden shops or other decorating outlets—beach sand may be polluted so use caution! It may be safer to buy landscape or decorative sand. Not only do decorative sands come in many colors but they are usually available in fine- or coarse-grain. If you're just beginning to work with sand, I recommend starting with a bag of white or natural-colored sand, as well as the black variety. This way, you're prepared for any type of spell. I usually use natural or white unless I'm banishing or binding. Buy one bag of fine-grain and one bag of coarse-grain so you can experiment with each type.

When it's time to dispose of sand you've used in a spell, avoid dumping large amounts into your yard (unless you're using it for a landscaping project). Sand is easy to recycle—you can use it in a dish for snuffing out matches or incense sticks. Remember, too, that when you layer sand it cannot be "un-layered" so if you remove it from the container it will be mixed. Again, find a way to recycle this sand if you no longer wish to use it for spells. I keep several containers reserved only for "used" sand—I use these mainly for burning non-magical candles and incense; I have one outside that is used as an ashtray for guests who smoke.

Since sand can be messy, work with it outside, if possible, or cover surfaces with newspaper. If you spill some, just vacuum it up. Aside from washing your hands, don't rinse sand down the drains inside your home. For storage, use glass jars with screw-top lids or large zipper-seal plastic bags. If you use bags, be sure the seal is tight—it's a hassle to clean up after a leaky bag of sand!

Other Magical Uses

Generally, I don't recommend using sand in spells for fertility or abundance, since very few things will grow in sand. While it's associated with the element of Earth and it can be a good additive for some soils (depending on the sand's mineral content), it's not particularly fertile. Rather, it is best used for burying, banishing, protection, spells involving impermanence, or in meditative spells involving creating something with sand or drawing in it.

First of all, sand is an excellent medium to use as a bed for stone grids (see chapter ten). You may wish to use damp sand for grids, especially if you're outside on a windy day. In addition, it's easier to draw lines and shapes in damp sand. Another method of drawing in sand involves setting a tray of dry sand outside and waiting for the symbol you created to blow away. Or, you can follow the Tibetan Buddhist tradition and ritually destroy what you created in the sand. Ceremonies of this type acknowledge the impermanence of things and can be used for dealing with grief or to affirm life.

To create objects, use a bit of water to dampen your sand as if you were going to build a sandcastle. Instead, pack your sand into cookie cutters to create shapes that pertain to your spell such as a heart or star. Remove the mold—this can be tricky. You'll need to practice to find the perfect amount of water so your sand isn't too wet or too dry. Take your sculpture outside and leave it until nature wears it down, either by rain or wind. You could also destroy it yourself in an act of banishing. Alternatively, use cookie cutters to make impressions in a bed of damp sand. When the sand dries, pour it back into a storage container. You may have to crumble it with your hands or sift it to remove clumps.

Have fun and be creative! You may already be familiar with sand art projects such as layering colored sand in bottles. Floral designers, too, know how pretty a design can become by combining sand, stones, shells, and glass beads or sea glass. You can design magical works of art or simply continue using sand as a burning base, knowing this can add to the magical significance of your work. Experiment with different grains and varying amounts of water. If you have kids, take them to the beach and do some "research" or build a sandbox. Even if you don't have a beach nearby or a sandbox, you can buy some sand, get some containers, and play!

Other Tips for Using Sand in Magic

- Create an "underwater landscape" for floating candles. Use a sand color that corresponds with your specific spell; add stones and shells. In general, coarse grain sand works better with water since the larger grains are heavier.

- When layering sand, you can put coarse on top of fine, but fine sand will simply fall in between the grains of coarse sand. So, unless you have uniform sand grains, remember to put fine on the bottom and coarse on top.

- Clean-up tip: For dry sand spells, dump the contents on a thin paper plate so you can easily pick out any stones or other objects. Then, crease the plate like a funnel and pour the sand into a storage container. For containers with water, pour the contents of your container in a place where you can easily separate the stones and glass but allow the sand to wash away—a place on the ground is best if you only have a small amount of sand, otherwise use a bucket or bowl.

- Experiment with sand depth. For instance, in a deep bowl, you can draw on top of the sand using a finely pointed object, such as the end of a feather, or a pencil. For shallow sand, you can trace thick lines that reveal the bottom of the container. Put a mirror under the sand so a reflective surface is revealed when you draw your shapes or, use colored plates or trays. Use sand art funnels or a folded sheet of paper to create fine lines.

- You may wish to buy some special tools to dedicate just for sand art such as cookie cutters, bowls, and plates. Clean them outside with a garden hose if possible. If not, brush off dry sand thoroughly before washing them in the sink or dishwasher.

Cleansing and Charging Sand

To cleanse sand, simply put it in a dish and cover it with enough water so it sits on top of the bed of sand. Let it sit in sunlight for a day, then pour the water off. Then, to complete the process and charge it, spread the damp sand onto a tray (you can use a cookie sheet or even a large plate) and let it dry in the sun for another day or until it's completely dry. This will clear it of any previous energy and you can dedicate it strictly for magical use. To charge dry sand, place your containers of sand in the sunlight or moonlight. If you purchase new sand from a craft store, you may skip the cleansing process the first time you use it; however, depending on what you use it for, you may wish to cleanse it before using it again. If you use the same sand for the same purpose over and over again, you don't need to keep cleansing and re-charging it—it's similar to the process of dedication. For example, keep a jar of black sand to only use for banishing and binding.

CLEANSING CHANT:
Sun and Water, clean this sand,
Clear the touch of other hands.

CHARGING CHANT:
Sun/Moon and Air, charge this sand,
Manifest the goal I've planned.

Sand and Stone Offering Bowl

Use this technique to create a special place to burn a candle or incense as an offering. Find a transparent glass dish and add sand, or layers of sand. Place one clear quartz point in the sand, along with a candle or a stick of incense to burn as your offering. You can use a tea light or votive in a glass cup, or you can simply place a votive candle in the sand. Cooled candle wax can be removed from sand easily.

VARIATION:
Use coarse sand, and pour water over it. Float a candle on top. Here's a general offering chant:

This offering I give with thanks,
Grateful and sincere.
For what I ask and have received,
For all that I hold dear.
Accept this gift, small as it seems—
Let my intent be clear.

Sand Spell for Banishing or Binding

You can use this spell for banishing, binding, or both. Remember that banishing is removing something from affecting you and binding is more like securing movement. Perform this spell during a waning moon.

STONES:

Your choice of the following: obsidian, or other type of volcanic glass or lava stone, black onyx, or lead (galena).

OTHER ITEMS:

• A glass container or jar, large enough to burn a candle in.

• Enough sand to nearly fill your container—For this spell, use black sand if you can find it; if not, use natural or white.

• A black candle—votive or tea light

Sprinkle a thin layer of sand in the bottom of the jar. The stone will represent that which is to be bound or banished (or both). Place the stone on the sand. Then, slowly, let sand fall from your fingertips (or use a funnel) onto the stone, eventually covering it.

Repeat this chant while visualizing your intended outcome:

That which causes me distress
That which keeps my mind from rest
For highest good be bound from me/
for highest good I banish thee
As I will, so mote it be.

When the stone is covered, place a black candle on top of the sand and light it.

CHANT:
By sand and stone, I cast this spell,
Air and Fire aid as well.
Hear my plea and heed my call,
I ask this for the good of all.

Allow the candle to burn out. Then, discard the wax and cleanse the stone. You can reuse the sand, but it's a good idea to only use it for future banishing or binding spells.

Sand Spell to Forget

Sometimes when a relationship is ending, we want to symbolically "erase" it from our lives. For this spell, create a "broken heart" shape in damp sand—you can either make a mold and draw a break across the center, or draw the entire shape in damp sand. For whatever method you choose, the goal is to create the symbol, then destroy it while visualizing any pain associated with the relationship being wiped away. Sand represents impermanence—nothing lasts forever. Your pain will heal with time. After you destroy the broken heart, by either using your hands or washing it with water, you can create a new, healed heart shape, if you wish.

Take some time and care creating your symbol. After all, you invested time in the relationship. Visualize being free and healed as you begin destroying your symbol.

CHANT:

Like wind and water on the sand,
Time brings changes to the land.
Pain and tears are wiped away—
Heal my heart; begin today.

Optional: Create a new, whole heart in the sand. Leave this one in place as long as you like.

Sand Protection Bottle

For this spell, get as creative as you like with the container and sand. Find an interesting bottle and use a funnel to pour differently colored sand in layers. Use any combination of colors you'd like or just stick to natural or white sand, if that's all you have available. Layering red, white, and black is one combination to try. You may wish to display this as a decorative item, or you can keep it hidden.

Somewhere in the bottle, place 9 grains of sea salt and a clear quartz point. You can put these on the bottom or in between layers.

CHANT:

With this bottle I prepare
Keep my home within your care.
All within and all without,
Everything I care about.
Harm to none I ask of thee,
As I will so shall it be.

Sacred Sand Spell

I once had the good fortune to witness Tibetan Buddhist monks create and destroy a sand mandala. It took them nearly a week to build it, and then it was ceremoniously wiped away. You can create your own similar ritual to honor life's magic and mystery. When the monks destroyed the mandala, they saved some of the sand. Most of it was dumped in a lake, but some was given to those of us who attended the ceremony. This sacred memento is a reminder that life is precious.

This spell assumes no level of artistic skill—I'm not going to ask you to create a sand art mandala! But, you can create a work of sand art and then destroy it. You can customize this spell based on your level of skill but this basic version is quite simple. It's the intent that matters.

SUPPLIES:

- two colors of sand—one white (or natural) and one black—of the same grain size

- a clear glass jar or bottle, any size

Begin this project at the full moon. Filling the container by alternating dark and light, making as many even layers of sand as you can (depending on the container's size). You can use a small votive cup or a large jar. Think of this as the symbolism of yin and yang—universal balance. As you add each layer of sand, chant:

Balance of life, dark and bright—
To make a shadow there must be light.

When the container is full, you can display it with a clear quartz point on top, seal the jar with a lid, or both. If possible, allow the jar to sit in moonlight on the first night. The next day, allow it to receive some sunlight so it can be charged this way as well. Then, place the container in a location where you can see it every day until the new moon. Chant these words over the container after you set it in place:

Massive stones can become sand,
Tiny grains can build a world.
Meaning found in simple things—
Let the magic be unfurled!

On the night of the new moon, repeat the chant above and pour the sand onto a plate. Swirl it around, and mix it in a counterclockwise direction.

CHANT:
To end is to begin again—
balance, swirl, mix, and blend.
Now I know and will transcend.
Understand: there is no end.

After the sand is mixed well, set some aside to keep. You can add a pinch of this sacred sand to other spells or just display in a decorative fashion. Discard the rest in a body of water.

VARIATION:
If you have coarse and fine sand, you can only make two layers, fine, then coarse. You can even make this on a tiny scale using a glass tealight cup and one layer of each color.

Glass Magic

While glass may seem commonplace to us today, it was once a product only for the wealthy. Making glass has become ordinary, although we still appreciate its beauty, especially in hand-blown works of art. We shouldn't forget how special hand-crafted items can be. I have several pieces of Murano glass jewelry I purchased on a trip to Italy, and even though they're not "natural" glass, they feel magical to me. Remember: glass comes from sand and sand is crushed minerals. While glass may be primarily manmade, it's still a natural, earthy substance. Many different kinds of glass are made today by adding various minerals to enhance the appearance.

Even though modern glass is manmade, nature makes glass as well. Specimens called fulgurites occur when lightning strikes sand (or a combination of sand, soil, and rock) and causes it to melt, creating a glasslike rod of fused minerals. If you are fortunate enough to have one of these, treasure it. Use it for glass magic if you like, but be careful—they're fragile. Obsidian and tachylyte (not as common) are types of volcanic glass that occur when magma cools by flowing into water. A formation called Pele's hair is a threadlike form of tachylyte.

Lead crystal is created by adding lead oxide to the mixture when making glass. This process originated in England in the seventeenth century. Waterford Crystal, made in Ireland, is one of the finest forms, but affordable lead crystal is easily obtained.

Remember that the terms "lead" crystal or "Austrian" crystal are used to describe types of glass and they have no crystalline structure. However, these manmade substances still have their place in magic. They're made of natural materials and are excellent choices for containers. Lead crystal prisms are easy to find and you can hang them in sunny areas to catch the light and throw rainbows around a room.

You probably already use glass for magic all the time—candle-holders are a primary example. They're affordable, attractive, and are available in all colors. We have glass dishes in our homes, glass beads for making jewelry, and don't forget about mirrors! Glass is everywhere, so it's easy to forget its magical significance. Charge your glass candleholders and mirrors as you would a stone or crystal, and continue to use them only for magical purposes. Dedicate specific containers for quarter candles and use specific jars and dishes for spells.

Sea Glass

While sea glass was originally a term specifically for water-worn bits of glass that washed up on seashores, it is now mostly manufactured for decorative purposes. If you happen to have some real sea glass, consider yourself lucky. If you don't, go ahead and buy some—it's lovely and can be used in glass magic.

Sea glass can be combined with sand and stones to create decorative containers that can also be charged for magical use. Select corresponding colors for your particular need—sea glass is often sold in bags of mixed colors.

Sea Glass Spell for Love

Use this spell to draw love into your life; perform on a Friday during a waxing or full moon.

ITEMS NEEDED:

- a glass bowl or dish

- a handful of sea glass in any color or combination—
  try to include some green, if possible

First, cleanse your dish and sea glass as you would a stone, clearing the pieces of previous energy. Place the sea glass in the dish and add enough water to cover. Use sea water if you have access to it, or try to find other clean water collected from a spring, lake, or stream.

After you have added the water, close your eyes and imagine feeling in love. Avoid thinking of a specific person—focus on the feeling of loving and being loved. Imagine this love is on a distant island separated from you by the sea. Then, sense the love coming closer to you like a bit of sea glass washed up on shore. See yourself walking on the beach, waiting, knowing this love is going to find you very soon. Hold your palms over the bowl of glass and water and say these words:

Love may be far or near—
When it's time, bring him/her here.
Water dries from this dish,
bring me love, grant my wish.

Place the bowl on your altar or in a windowsill until the water has evaporated. Begin watching for signs that your spell is manifesting.

Austrian Crystal Sun Catcher

The goal of this spell is to create a decorative sun catcher intended to promote happiness and a positive attitude. Austrian crystals are faceted to sparkle in the light—choose any shape you'd like—a star, heart, snowflake, pyramid—you will most likely find dozens to choose from; they're typically drilled with a hole at the top to be hung or used in jewelry.

THREE METHODS:

1. The simplest way to use the crystal as a sun catcher is to thread a piece of string through it, tie the ends of the

string in a knot, and hang it in a window. That's really all you need to do. But, since it may be difficult to add additional beads to string or ribbon (depending on size), you may want to just use the crystal. Done!

2. If you want to incorporate additional beads, the easiest way to string beads is to use bead wire. But, if you do this, you can't just tie a knot in the end, you'll need to use crimp beads to secure it. Still, this is one of the first steps to learn in jewelry-making and it's an easy technique. You only need to buy one tool, some crimp beads, and bead wire. Just visit your local craft store and they'll be happy to assist you. You could also purchase a book or look up techniques online.

3. If you'd like to experiment with jewelry-making techniques or you already have all the tools and supplies, try the Bead and Crystal Star Sun Catcher described here. And of course, you can create your own design.

These techniques and this project are by no means intended to limit what you can do—rather, I want to show you three basic projects so you can create your own version.

After selecting your crystal, choose additional beads based on your need and/or numerological influence (see chapter nine). You don't have to follow this design, it's just a suggestion.

BEAD AND CRYSTAL STAR SUN CATCHER:

- one very small star-shaped Austrian crystal

- five faceted red glass beads

- five round clear quartz beads

- bead stringing wire, crimp beads, various jewelry-making tools

- Optional: silver chain or cord; other decorative jewelry-making supplies

This example is based on fives: five of each bead and a five-pointed star. In numerology, five is the number of life itself. Another variation would be to use four different colored beads that correspond to the elements, and let the Austrian crystal piece represent the Spirit.

When I made this one, I used a strand of bead wire and put the crystal star on first, then pushed the bead wire back through it. I added a silver crimp bead to secure the star in place. Then, I had a double-strand of wire to use for the other beads—I alternated red and clear. After adding all the beads, I put another silver crimp bead at the top, leaving a loop so I could hang this piece from a chain.

I added some other decorative touches to the one I made—I put a silver tube bead over the top crimp bead to hide it and attached a large silver loop at the very top so I could easily change the sun catcher is hung. I can string a silver chain through it or use a cord or ribbon. The crystal star I used is only about half an inch wide, and since this sun catcher is small, it could even be hung from the rearview mirror of a car.

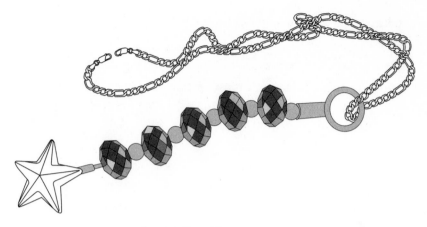

Austrian Crystal Star Sun Catcher

Remember—if you don't have all the tools and supplies, simply hang your crystal from a string or ribbon. Charge your sun catcher in sunlight, on a Sunday, if possible. Here's a general chant to empower it:

Crystal, catch the light of sun,
sparkle in the air,
keep the brightness in my life,
with me everywhere.
Let me always see the light,
let it be my guide,
knowing hope will shine for me,
show me the bright side.

Visualize the crystal and beads soaking up the sun's energy. Allow it to catch the rays and sparkle and reflect—see if you can get rainbows to project on the walls. Imagine the sunlight being kept in these beads and crystal bringing you joy and happiness when you look at it, even on a cloudy day.

Of course, you can also further customize your sun catcher for a specific goal. They're also fun cat toys—they love to chase the rainbows!

- SIX -

ELEGANT EARTH MAGIC: THE UNEXPECTED POWER OF ROCKS

Introduction

Rocks are the cake of which pure minerals are the ingredients. Therefore, an "ordinary" rock can be a powerful combination of many crystals with powerful metaphysical properties. Seemingly simple rocks that you find can become important magical tools, evoking emotion and memory. When you travel, try to find a rock as a souvenir (but be aware there are certain places that prohibit this). Rocks found near water that are polished smooth or have holes worn through can also be especially meaningful as symbols of the power of the natural elements. These can also be used to represent places where they were found, such as oceans, lakes, or rivers. I have several stones collected from various vacations—from local camping and float trips to pieces picked up on beaches in California, Mexico, and Jamaica—even a favorite rock I found in Greece. Each one is a token of remembrance. One very special rock in my collection is one I found in the woods of my childhood home. It's just a chunk of granite, but it contains glittering chips of garnet and pyrite. It's a treasured piece that not only holds special memories of my home, but it can be used for the minerals' metaphysical properties.

In addition, fossils can become priceless parts of your collection; you can search for them on your own or purchase them. You don't need to know exactly what it is or how old (unless you want to research it)—simply knowing it's a remnant of life from millions of years ago is wondrous. For use in magic, you can consider the mineral content of your fossil if you'd like, but I prefer to give less consideration to that and more to what kind of specimen you have: plant or animal. Find out as much as you can about it. Do some research on your own and you should be able to determine what it is.

Some legends say supernatural beings reside in rocks. In parts of India, small mounds of stones are erected to represent goddesses that protect villages. The ancient Greeks would leave piles of stones alongside roads in honor of Hermes, god of travel and communication, as protection on the journey. In Delphi, a stone (the omphalos) was said to mark the center of the world. Some ancient mysteries speak of stones as the powdered bones of Saturn, forming the spirits of human beings. Rocks are considered to be the bones of the great mother, Gaea, and Scandinavian myths say stones and cliffs are the bones of Ymir. Rocks have been valued as long as humans have existed.

And, of course, the use of stones for spiritual and mystical purposes abounds throughout the world at places like Stonehenge, Carnac, and various cairns and other structures, some used to mark time, like a calendar, or to designate sacred places. Accounts of sacred stones occur in nearly every spiritual path.

Stone Healing Circles

Many cultures have used circles of stone and other types of layouts for various spiritual purposes. I will not attempt to create a version of the medicine wheels of American Indian traditions, but if you have experience with this it can be incorporated into your crystal magical practice. If not, it's easy to create your own tradition of stone healing circles. Here's one idea to get you started.

Begin by choosing a photo or symbol to represent someone who needs to receive healing energy. (There is a self-healing spell later in this chapter.) Next, build a circle of rocks around the symbol, visualizing the rocks as a wall, a safe haven.

CHANT:
Healing stones, circle round,
Linking cosmos and the ground.
Offer strength and all be well,
Hear me as I cast this spell.

State your specific purpose.

VARIATIONS:

- In your selection of rocks for the circle, granite would be a good choice. You can also incorporate the person's personal power stone, if you know it—that stone can be used in the center to represent the person in need or just be one of the rocks in the circle, or both (chapter eight contains more information on personal power stones). I like to place the individual's personal power stone on top of a photo. In addition, you can select specific stones from the Appendix that have qualities you wish to draw upon.

- To create a meaningful symbolic or magical stone to carry, paint or draw a symbol or rune on a rock and charge it inside a stone circle. Then, carry it with you.

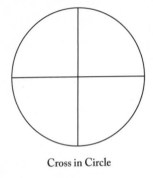

Cross in Circle

Four Quarters

This is a symbol that's quite common, especially in many American Indian traditions, representing the four directions. This is sometimes used to represent a crossroads or the Earth. Much like we use the pentagram to represent the four elements and spirit, this, too, can be used to represent the world. Use this symbol in circle casting by creating it on an altar and calling the quarters. You can place the stones on the altar itself or, create a cross shape on a plate of sand and place a stone for each direction.

Face each direction and chant as you place each quarter stone:

I greet the East, the sun will rise,
the force of air, the breath of skies;

I greet the South, intense and bright,
the strength of fire, to pierce the night;

I greet the West, the rain and sea,
the might of water, comforts me;

I greet the North, the tree and stone,
the weight of Earth, I'm not alone.

Construct this image from various rocks in whatever size you desire.

This circle can also be used to represent the four seasons, using corresponding stones of your choice. In addition, you can add a stone to the center to represent spirit or Mother Earth—a geode would be an excellent choice. You can build this circle using stones you find in your area, adding local significance to it. This circle would be appropriate for any seasonal celebration and it can easily be built by a group during a ritual.

Spell for Unity and Wholeness

This spell is loosely based on the idea of Squaring the Circle (see chapter ten). In *Man and His Symbols*, psychologist Carl Jung refers to the concept of squaring the circle as "one of the many archetypal motifs which form the basic patterns of our dreams and fantasies ...Indeed, it could even be called the archetype of wholeness."

For this ritual, create the figure in the diagram using any collection of rocks. Imagine the large outer circle is the cosmos and the center circle is the moon. The square represents your earthly perspective—you are united with the cosmos. This represents a unity of spirit and matter, earth and moon.

In the center, place an object (represented by the black dot) that represents you—this could be a stone (perhaps a geode) or even a tarot card, picture, or other item.

Visualize your connection with the earth, moon, and the cosmos.

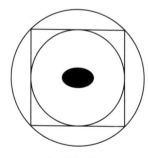

Spell for Unity
and Wholeness

CHANT:

*All I am and will become
is in my reach, it is the sum
of all I am and all I've done;
what I wish, I will become.
Part of whole and every part
is in my body, soul, and heart,
with the universe I'm one—
by earth and sky, by moon and sun.*

Stone's Throw Spell

The familiar phrase "a stone's throw away" is used to suggest a close distance. This spell is intended to set a goal in motion by throwing a stone—knowing that your goal is close at hand—it's literally a stone's throw away and not out of reach, even if it feels like a distant dream. This spell is good to initiate a new beginning or to reestablish an ongoing goal you may have.

Use any rock; perform during a new or waxing moon.

Find a safe place to throw the stone—either on your property or in a wilderness area. Use a small stone, one you are comfortable throwing. Remember to be sure there is nothing in the way that the stone could hit or damage.

As you throw the stone, visualize the journey to your goal—it's only as far as you can throw the rock. Remember, you're not throwing it away, you're seeing a distance that is closer than you realize. Give the stone a toss, and chant:

> *Stone I throw, now you show*
> *The goal that I beseech.*
> *Not too far, I know you are*
> *Never out of reach.*

VARIATION: ROCK RELEASE SPELL

An alternate form of this spell is to throw a stone into a body of water to "release" something in your life. Perform during a waning moon phase, visualize what you're releasing being lost in the water, and use this chant:

> *Stone I throw, I let go—*
> *This, I now release.*
> *Travel far, I know you are*
> *Safely out of reach.*

Anchor Spell

Use this spell any time you feel you are drifting from a goal or you feel the need to hold yourself in place. This is similar to grounding, but more related to a specific place or goal that you want to hold on to. This spell is best used to increase determination when you feel lack of motivation. However, realize that there is a time to let go of some things—you may wish to use a divination technique first to be sure you're on the right path.

Use any stone to represent your anchor. You may wish to choose one that's large and heavy. Find a place to leave this stone where it won't be moved. As you place the stone, visualize it as an anchor to your goal or a symbol of your will and determination.

CHANT:

Firm and strong, anchor stone,
standing though the winds have blown.
Holding fast, despite the waves,
Keep me fixed, resolved and brave.

Wishing Spell

For this spell, use any type of rock. Find a place where you can bury it—in your yard or in a potted plant. Hold the stone in your projective hand and visualize your wish. Imagine that wish being inscribed onto the stone. Then, imagine the stone as a seed and plant it—your wish will be nurtured by the soil and will grow. Chant as you bury the stone:

Like a seed my wish will grow,
For the good of all I know.
This I need and do deserve,
As the symbol rock will serve.

Stone Spell for Healing

Earth magic often involves healing and nurturing—use this spell when you are in need of healing energy. Use any combination of fossils and/or pieces of petrified wood. Place the stones in a glass jar filled with soil—you can use potting soil if you'd like. Arrange the stones so you can see them through the jar. Consider the stones: the fossils reveal evidence of ancient life on Earth; petrified wood (which is actually "fossilized") was once a living organism as well—an ancient tree. If you don't have any fossils or petrified wood, use amber or jet—these are "organic" stones. You can make this arrangement as small or as large as you wish.

Visualize the ancient energy of the stones—they have endured. See this timeless flow filling you with healing and comfort.

CHANT:
Ancient life of long ago,
Evidence I see in stone.
Secrets only time reveals
As the earth sustains and heals.
Endurance of the tree that towers,
By these stones I am empowered.

Leave the stones in place until you feel the spell has manifested.

VARIATION:
If you prefer, bury the stone(s) in a potted plant instead of a jar.

Stone for Safe Travel

For this spell you will need one small rock from your home: your yard, garden, driveway, any ordinary stone—but it must be one found where you live, in the ground your home is on (not one you purchased or found elsewhere). You will take this with you on your trip; it's a link to your home.

Hold the stone and visualize it as your home foundation. Imagine a safe and enjoyable journey, and see yourself back home again. Use this chant:

> *Tiny stone, piece of home*
> *Keep me safe as I roam.*

Carry this rock with you on your trip. When you get home, return the rock to the place where you found it or keep it as part of your collection for stone magic and use it again next time you travel.

Geodes

No discussion of using rocks in magic would be complete without mentioning geodes. Geodes can be used in magic to represent the womb of the earth. They can also be used to symbolize unity, "the big picture," or wholeness. The name *geode* comes from the Greek and actually means "earthlike." Geodes can be very tiny or impressively large (I have one that's half an inch in diameter and one that's almost a foot) and they are a must-have for your collection.

Often the base stone is a sedimentary type, like limestone, and the center is quartz or some variety of chalcedony, like banded agate. Sometimes the center is solid crystal rather than a hollow cavity. You may have seen these in stores—often they are cut in half and polished—sometimes sold as a set to use as bookends or other decorative items. While they appear uninteresting on the outside, the center is like an amazing crystal cave.

Geodes can take thousands of years to form, the result of a special combination of pressure, water, and minerals. It begins with a cavity of some kind—sometimes a shell or a bubble of gas in magma. A salty solution becomes trapped inside; the outside eventually dissolves or fossilizes and the cavity is preserved. As water seeps in and out, layers of deposits are built up, lining the cavity. When this stone shell cracks, more minerals and water seep in, forming crystals in the cavity. Depending on the minerals involved, the crystals can be clear quartz, amethyst, calcite, or others. If the crystals grow to fill the entire cavity, a nodule is formed. If a hollow space remains, it becomes a geode.

You may be able to find these on your own—round or egg-shaped stones—and break them open to reveal the treasure inside. Most likely, however, you will purchase these at a store. I like to find whole ones that still fit together. Sometimes the halves are sliced perfectly and polished. Be aware that polished geodes sold in stores are sometimes artificially dyed with bright colors.

Geode Spell for Secrets

Ever have a secret you feel you just have to tell? Whisper it into the cavity of a geode and visualize it being absorbed into the stone. You can use this method as a type of conversation with the earth—to seek the answer to a question or problem or to speak a fear or secret desire. Imagine the earth holding it, nurturing you, and offering healing if necessary. After you tell your secret, use this chant to seal it:

Stone, please keep my secret safe,
Trust I place in you.
Answer if you can, if not—
Hold it and be true.

You can bury the stone if you like, or keep it in sight—depending on your situation and personal preference. When you feel an appropriate time has passed, cleanse the stone to clear it and visualize the secret washing away with the water.

– SEVEN –

SPECIAL QUARTZ POINTS

Introduction

I'll always remember the first clear quartz point I acquired. I was around nine years old; my family and I were touring a local cave—one of many we have in Missouri. There in the gift shop, I found a tiny double-terminated point. Examining it more closely now, this point also has a place in the center where it appears it once intersected with another crystal—it looks like the stone was broken here at one time, but seems to have repaired itself. Metaphysically, this is a "self-healed" crystal. Once I learned more about these special types of points, I had to study each one in my collection to discover its characteristics.

You are probably familiar with the various types of special quartz points cited in many crystal magic reference books. Here I will explore some of the most popular forms and ways you can use them. In addition, I have included a dedication you can use for each type. The descriptions in this chapter refer mainly to clear quartz, although you may find them in other colors of quartz and other types of minerals. Where these formations occur in types of quartz other than the clear variety the properties of that crystal also apply. For example, an amethyst record keeper may have a deeper spiritual potential than clear quartz, or perhaps it has other lessons to teach that involve addiction or anxiety.

Irregularities that occur during crystal formation create fascinating specimens. You'll find hundreds of terms to explain these variations—some describe the unique growth pattern of the crystal; some have been created with New Age practices. There are far too many to cover here, so don't get too caught up with all the different types. Just remember that these formations give the crystals a "personality" or specific characteristic we can use in our metaphysical practice. And, naturally, there are specimens that defy category. In fact, we can probably create a special category for just about every type of shape that exists—everything from points that appear to be gently fused together to those that seem to have collided with each other. The combinations of markings are almost endless. In this chapter, we'll take a closer look at a few of the most popular forms of quartz points: the window crystal, the generator, channeling crystal, double-terminated point, Isis point, self-healed crystal, "rainbow" crystals, and the record keeper. The chants provided can be used to help you cleanse and dedicate your crystals. Once you notice these different faces and features, you'll be compelled to examine every point you have and the ones you buy in the future. You just might find some unique specimens in your collection you didn't even know you had.

Many crystals are chipped at the top so they don't reach a perfect point. These are still fine to use in magic. Sometimes you can find irregular or flawed quartz points for a bargain price—these are great to have on hand for creating grids (see chapter ten). Most crystal points are not perfectly water-clear. In fact, inclusions and imperfections make some very interesting specimens.

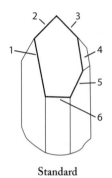

Standard
Quartz Point

First let's consider the standard quartz point. They usually have six sides on the base and six faces on the point. The faces are almost always of irregular shape and size and often one face will dominate and be largest. Sometimes the other faces can be very tiny. Each "face" of the point has sides of a varying number—count the lines—there will usually be from three to seven, sometimes eight. This is one of the features that determine many of the special points listed in this chapter.

Window Crystal

Window Crystal

These crystals have one or more diamond-shaped "windows" where the base meets the point. In some cases, the window is a stretched rectangle, not a diamond shape. These are often called windows to the future (leaning forward) or past (leaning back), or "timelines" so you can contemplate and explore what to learn from the past and what to prepare for in the future. Some sources refer to these stretched "rectangular windows" as activation points that can be used to help stimulate left and right brain functions. However you decide to use them, these window crystals can help attune your mind and insight.

Window crystals are good to use in divination—hold them while you read tarot cards or keep with your deck. They are useful for engaging your third eye and excellent for self-reflection and contemplation. Try sleeping with one under your pillow to gain insight from dreams. Before using your window crystal for a specific purpose, dedicate it by visualizing your need and focusing your intent.

CHANT:

Window help me see, make it crystal clear,
Window let me know, allow it to appear.

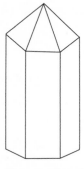

Generator Crystal

Generator Crystal

On these crystals are six (almost even) faces that meet at a point. These are rare in nature and are often cut and polished to form a perfect point. These cut stones may still be used and are not inferior to natural ones, although it certainly is special to find a natural generator. The cut ones are usually shaped so they can stand on their own on a flat base, with the point directed upward. Some natural generator points are polished, too, to accentuate the crystal faces. It's useful to have a couple of different types for your collection.

Generator points are intended to magnify and evenly direct energy flow, so they're also a good addition to a grid (chapter ten) or other layout. Consider placing one in the center of a group ritual to help project the raised energy—first pass the stone around the group so everyone has a chance to hold it. Often these types are used as wand points, but you can simply hold them in your hand to aid in directing energy.

To dedicate your generator point, hold it in your projective hand and visualize the energy flowing from within you, through your arm, hand, fingertips, and finally, through the crystal, where the energy picks up power and is focused into a beam—a beam that emanates from the point like a laser. Use this same visualization when using the crystal. During dedication, use this chant:

Through my body and the stone,
energy we share, not own,
flowing forth with pure intent,
with this stone my will is sent.

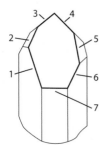

Channeling Crystal

Channeling Crystal

These points have one large face on the point that has seven flat edges. Ideally, there should be a triangular face on the opposite side. Some generator points have perfect symmetry—three faces with seven sides and, in between, three faces with three sides. Since this crystal is associated with the number seven, it is perfect for mystical and spiritual pursuits, and it can be used to help you gain wisdom from within as well as without.

If generator points send energy and help with the flow, channeling points are used to receive energy—these are especially well-suited for meditation that is focused on a specific issue. I have a large channeling point that happens to be smoky quartz. I find this type especially useful for meditation.

USES FOR A CHANNELING CRYSTAL:

- To open a channel to receive energy or information (while awake or dreaming)

- To enter a meditative state

- To activate your third eye

Hold the stone against your third eye (use your receptive hand) or point it toward you; be open to accepting whatever insight you receive. Listen.

Moonlight is especially effective for charging a channeling point. Here's a chant to get you started:

For good of all I will allow,
Let the way be open now.
I accept and I believe
that what I need I will receive.

Double-Terminated Crystal

These crystals have a point on each end, and while they're often carved this way for pendants, you should be able to find some natural ones. These points are good choices for use in astral projection, meditation, and for dream magic. Try sleeping with one of these in your pillowcase to receive the answer to a question. In addition, these crystals are sometimes used as pendulums. Try this chant to get the energy moving:

Double-
Terminated
Crystal

Flowing forth and back again,
energy both out and in.
As I need and do intend,
energy receive and send.

These points are excellent choices for use in grids (chapter ten) since they increase the flow of energy. These can also be used between two people or in groups to facilitate the movement of energy.

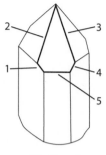

Isis Crystal

Isis Crystal

This is one of the more difficult point variations to find. In this case, the largest face on the point has five sides arranged in a very specific shape (see Figure 9). The lines don't need to be perfect, but the shape still needs to be present. Use this point to get in touch with your inner goddess—it contains strong feminine energy.

Since this crystal is associated with the number five, it is also useful in spells for healing, comfort, dealing with emotional issues, fertility, and love (see chapter nine for other numerological associations). This is the best of female power, nurturing and strong. Use this chant to attune to this energy:

Strong and wise, goddess rise,
help me see, with your eyes.

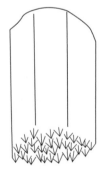

Self-Healed Crystal

Self-Healed Crystal

There are two main types of self-healed crystals. One type appears to have been broken and then grown back together again. These types usually display a cloudy area where the fracture occurred and the point may no longer be perfectly straight. Sometimes the growth changes angles and the crystal looks crooked. The other type of self-healed or regrown crystal lacks the jagged bottom where it was separated from its base. Instead, it has a smooth base with the emergence of several triangular points. There may be dozens or even hundreds of these; they may resemble record keeper points layered on top of one another. In this case, after the point was broken from its base, it experienced a chance to begin growth again.

These self-healed points are good for any type of healing work. Hold these in your hand or place them on the area where you wish to receive healing energy. Visualize the specific healing you need and repeat this chant:

Renew, repair, heal with care.

You can also wrap these in a cloth and conceal them beneath your clothes, if you wish, or find a way to wear them as jewelry.

"Rainbow" Crystals

Sometimes when you turn a specimen into the light a certain way, bands or swirls of colors often resembling rainbows appear inside the stone. This is caused by a fracture inside the crystal (sometimes these form as the crystal is growing; sometimes they are caused during the mining process). These "flaws" often create a lovely appearance. Meditate with rainbow crystals for spirituality or to increase joy and happiness.

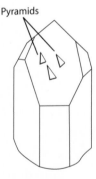

Pyramids

Record Keeper
Crystal

Record Keeper Crystal

Cited as one of the most mystical and rare of special crystal forms, record keepers have tiny triangles on one or more of the crystal faces. These markings can vary from easily visible, prominently raised shapes to ones that are so smooth they're almost impossible to see unless you're looking for them. Record keepers are said to store ancient knowledge; some say they hold the secrets of the universe if one can but unlock them. Whatever the reason for these triangles, they are rare and exciting to find.

My experience with record keepers began with one large clear point and one amethyst cluster. I wasn't looking for them—they "found" me, as record keepers often do. I didn't know the clear point was a record keeper when I bought it; I purchased it at a rock swap, along with several other points that were being sold at a very low price because they were "flawed." In this case, the triangles are very small and subtle; some of the faces of this point are rough and scaly, probably the reason it was considered imperfect.

My amethyst record keeper was given to me by a fellow rock enthusiast. This particular amethyst cluster contains hematite giving the stone a rusty, reddish-brown appearance (sometimes called red amethyst). It turns out that at least four of the points in this cluster are record keepers!

Allow me to digress for a moment to share a record keeper story.

One day I noticed my red amethyst record keeper cluster had accumulated quite a bit of dust; it had been sitting on a shelf and had become neglected. After I had carefully cleaned it, I spent some time with it that day, meditating. I realized that I had never fully appreciated this stone because of its unusual color.

Later that night, I picked up my most recently acquired quartz point. Exactly one month prior, I obtained this gorgeous specimen in a trade. It was my first Isis point; a clear point that's almost nine inches long. I just happened to turn the point into the light and suddenly discovered it was a record keeper! It had a few very tiny triangles on several of the facets, and I never noticed before.

Maybe my eyes were better trained or maybe it was the angle of the light, but I then decided to recheck all my other quartz points. I've had some of these points for decades, crystals that I've studied and worked with many times. Sure enough, three of them turned out to be record keepers! How could it be that I never noticed? Perhaps it's true that these special points are made known to someone when they need to receive knowledge. Or, perhaps my work with one of them earlier that day activated my awareness, or activated the stones. Whatever the reason, I'm delighted to have these stones to work with.

The lessons to take away from this experience are: give your crystals some time—it may take years for you to be ready for what they have to offer; revisit your stones periodically to clean and study them; and pay attention to subtle signs.

When you're trying to identify a record keeper, first wipe the stone clean with a soft cloth. Be sure there are no fingerprints on it. Turn the crystal facets so light shines across them creating an almost mirror-like surface; examine every side of the point. Unlike the more obvious raised triangles, you won't see this type of marking if you look at the crystal straight-on. Also, you may want to use a magnifying glass if you have very small points to examine. And remember that sometimes the triangles are almost like an outline drawn on the crystal—you won't be able to feel them with your finger. You may find a single triangle, or dozens, or more than you can count. Sometimes they even overlap each other. They may appear on only one face or several.

Another interesting feature among my record keepers is that of the six I have, three of them were acquired without the exchange of money— they were either gifts or obtained through trade. Of these three, two are extra special: the red amethyst cluster and the Isis point; the others are regular clear points—they don't have any other special characteristics. I believe this is significant because it shows that sometimes stones that "find" you are often extraordinary and really do have a purpose. It may take years for you to realize it, but keep an eye on those stones—their purpose will eventually be revealed to you. You may even have some of them right now and aren't yet aware of their presence.

Here's another interesting point to note. Three of my clear quartz record keepers are self-healed at the base. The base of each has numerous triangle shapes stacked together. In my collection of more than thirty clear quartz points, only these three record keepers display the self-healing pattern. Obviously, these shapes are part of the natural crystal growth pattern but it made me wonder: perhaps this type of self-healed crystal has something to do with the formation of record keeper crystals. So, check the base of your points and, if you see these self-healed markings, check the facets of the point to see if you have a record keeper. A self-healed record keeper could hold even more power and insight for the user. And if your self-healed record keeper has other special features it's truly a treasure. Whatever the reason for these little pyramids, they're interesting and rare.

To "activate" your record keeper, you can try several approaches. Meditate with it, sleep with it near you or under your pillow, or carry it with you. Hold the stone and rub the tiny triangles with your finger or fingernail. Be open to receiving messages. Try this chant:

Mystic shape of lines beneath my touch,
make your secret knowledge known to me.
Help me learn the wisdom that I seek—
let me know what I am meant to see.

Visualize the tiny triangles opening up to reveal information. You can also use this stone to work with your third eye chakra, visualizing your ability to "see" what the crystal has to reveal. Hold the stone to your forehead if you wish. You can imagine one of the triangles as a doorway—walk through it.

– EIGHT –

RITUALS, MEDITATIONS, AND AFFIRMATIONS

Introduction

Throughout my experience working with stones, I've found that meditation is one of the most useful techniques. There's something comforting about holding a stone, or gazing upon it—it can help us relax and quiet our minds. The spells in this chapter are united by their use in meditation, divination, or use for a type of dedication or personal affirmation ritual.

Ritual to Dedicate Your Personal Power Stone

What is a personal power stone? These are stones that individuals are attracted to, often for reasons they can't explain. We may say we are initially drawn to them because of their appearance, but sometimes we want to have a stone because our insight tells us we need it. Use all these reasons to explore finding your personal power stones. Similar to animal totems, these stones may change for us over periods of time, and we may have several that we use for particular times in our lives. Use your intuition; meditate. Research the qualities of the stone you have selected. You may discover a need you have not addressed and you can then learn ways to use your personal power stones to enrich your life. (See chapter nine for suggestions based on birth month, zodiac, and numerology.)

How You Can Tell if a Stone Is a Personal Power Stone:

- You more than just "like" it. You feel compelled to acquire several shapes or pieces of jewelry. You have several sizes and styles of the same stone.

- People give them to you, or you seem to acquire them easily. These stones tend to "find" you. You may or may not actually feel drawn to them.

If you do feel drawn to a stone, that's also a sign. Or it could be a sign that you simply think it's an attractive stone. Not every stone you wear needs to be a personal power stone. Gems and stones are still used for decoration, after all!

We all choose stones we think are pretty for jewelry or decorative purposes. But sometimes we just "need" a stone for no reason we can explain. Do not ignore this insight—you apparently need this particular stone at this time for a reason.

I have a close friend and coven sister who has never liked the color pink. However, she found herself inexplicably drawn to a lovely specimen of rose-colored rhodochrosite (which is not a stone associated with her astrological sign or birth month). No matter that this was a stone she considered out of character for her, she wanted it—needed it. She described a calming and soothing feeling that came over her the first time she held it. This is one example of being drawn to a stone—especially one that normally wouldn't catch your interest.

My friend eventually purchased some beads made of rhodochrosite to make a necklace. It turns out that this is a personal power stone for her. She stumbled upon it quite by accident, or so it appears. Always listen to your inner voice.

As another example, I recently attended a gem and mineral show with a good friend who is a collector but does not usually work with the metaphysical aspect of stones. She wondered why she was always drawn to particular types of stones or why certain stones always seemed to "find" her. Our discussion revealed that she had been practicing chakra work for opening her third eye and using her intuition. It's not surprising that amethyst was one of the stones she was attracted to.

To learn from your personal power stone, meditate with it, wear it, sleep with it under your pillow or carry it with you. Research its metaphysical properties and folklore. See if there's anything that corresponds with current situations in your life. If you don't see an immediate connection that's OK, something may come up in the future that you need to be prepared for. Or you may just need to strengthen a particular area of your life.

You can dedicate any type of personal power stone (raw or tumbled stones, jewelry, or carved shapes) by using this ritual.

Place the stone on your altar or other sacred space, visualize a bond between you and the stone, and chant:

Stone of mine, you came to me
Stone divine, I ask of thee
On this day, at this hour
I seek to find distinctive power;
What you have in store for me
For good of all so shall it be.

Ritual for Opening Your Third Eye

The third eye is known as the seat of intuition and insight; it's also the location of one of the chakras. Use this ritual to practice seeking wisdom and learning to use your intuition. Begin by selecting a stone from this list—these are all reputed to aid the opening of the third eye: amethyst, apatite, apophyllite, azurite, fluorite (purple), Herkimer diamond, iolite, kyanite, lapis lazuli, moonstone, opal, clear quartz, wulfenite.

Breathe deeply and center yourself. Visualize your third eye opening—imagine an actual eye in the center of your forehead, granting insight and focusing your natural psychic ability. Hold the stone to your forehead while you visualize and chant:

Eye that sees
All there is
Open wide
Nothing hides
Eye that knows
Eye that shows
What I need
Now is freed.

Smoky Quartz Spell for Temperance

Smoky quartz has been called the "stone of cooperation." It can be used to help remove emotional and mental blocks, transform negativity, and aid balancing and grounding techniques. Because of these characteristics, smoky quartz is good for adding clarity and depth to meditation while at the same time allowing you to be "present" in your physical body—use it to get in touch with yourself—physically and mentally.

I have always been drawn to smoky quartz—perhaps it's because I'm a Libra, and the balancing nature of this crystal calls to me. For meditation,

I can't recommend this stone highly enough. Because it's quartz, it helps clear the mind yet it has a calming and soothing element. It grounds, but not too much, leaving the mind free to expand. I also like to hold this crystal before and after yoga. It has a gentle energy that's perfect for preparing and relaxing the body. That's why I think this stone is perfect for temperance—it has a balance of grounding and uplifting—leaving one feeling centered, calm, and content. Moderation allows you to enjoy the pleasure of an experience without over-indulging—a useful practice for anyone who has bad habits or the tendency to enjoy too much of a good thing. Because of these gently balancing qualities, smoky quartz has been noted astrologically as a stone especially suited for those born in Libra. However, anyone can receive the benefits smoky quartz offers. This spell works with the balancing aspect of the stone to help one achieve moderation.

Naturally, if you have an addiction or medical condition you should seek the assistance of a licensed professional. Consider using this ritual in accordance with a management program. If you have a bad habit you want to curb, use this spell to help you achieve balance and strength.

For this particular spell, the best type of smoky quartz to use is a point or tumbled piece. Jewelry can work as well, but an unset stone held in your hand will generate the most energy. Of course, charging a piece of smoky quartz jewelry during this spell will help keep the energy present with you after the ritual. Perform during a waning or dark moon; the moon in the sign of Libra is ideal.

In addition to the piece of smoky quartz (combined with a piece of smoky quartz jewelry, if you choose) you will need:

- table or altar

- two candles—one black and one white

Sit on the floor facing a small altar or meditation table, or sit on a chair near a table. Light a black candle and a white candle on the table in front of you and place the stone between them.

Visualize the balance you strive for. Then, pick up the stone (and put on the piece of jewelry) in both of your hands. Repeat this chant six times:

Balance of the dark and light,
balance I seek on this night.
Faced with choice, I pass the test—
find the balance that is best.

Meditate as long as you like, holding the stone and gazing at the candles. When you feel ready, replace the stone between the candles and allow the candles to burn out. Hold the stone whenever you feel the need, and/or wear the piece of jewelry. Repeat this spell as desired every few months.

Dream Spell

This spell can serve a variety of purposes. Perhaps you wish to remember your dreams, hope for a prophetic dream to give insight into a problem, or maybe you want to dispel nightmares. You'll need a chunk of celestite, the larger the better. This is the best stone to use for dream magic—it's also good for balance and problem solving, and it can aid astral travel. You will keep this stone under your bed or on a bedside table. If you have a small, smooth stone, you could place it beneath your pillow or in your pillowcase, if you'd like.

Dedicate the stone. Visualize the stone magnifying your dreams, clarifying them, helping them to stay with you, and, most importantly, allowing you to gain access to their meaning.

CHANT:

Dreaming state, elusive thoughts, mysteries of night,
Bring me knowledge, wonder, peace, as I dream tonight.

Prayer Beads

The word *bead* comes to us from the Anglo-Saxon *bidden*, a word meaning "to pray," and *bede*, meaning "prayer." These beads are considered "all-purpose" because they generally cover things often focused upon in prayer and can be used as a general framework for most personal needs and expression.

Once again you have the option of using jewelry-making skills and tools for a project. If you don't have the tools or supplies, string the beads on thread, tying each end in a secure knot.

YOU WILL NEED:

- 1 piece of clear quartz, drilled for stringing, pendant style (or, you may decide to use a crystal point, or another symbol such as a goddess figure, pentacle, etc.)

- 5 sterling silver beads (any size, preferably smaller than the prayer beads)

- 2 round hematite beads

- 3 round clear quartz beads

- 5 round tiger eye beads

- 8 round aventurine beads

- 13 round rose quartz beads

For best results, keep the beads to a uniform size. However, the first set (hematite and clear quartz) may be smaller than the others, if desired.

String the beads on wire as follows: After the main piece, add a silver bead, then the 2 hematite, 3 clear quartz, another silver bead, 5 tiger eye, another silver, 8 aventurine, another silver, then the 13 rose quartz, and the final silver. Seal the strand any way you like. I used the final silver bead to crimp the strand. Tip: don't string the beads so tightly that they won't move at all. Let your strand be a bit flexible so you can slide the beads very slightly beneath your fingers. You can tie a ribbon or tassel on the end, if you'd like.

The numbers of stones correspond to the Fibonacci Sequence: 1, 2, 3, 5, 8, and 13. The stones are used for the following purposes: Clear quartz is a good overall energy amplifier and the silver acts to conduct the energy through the strand. Hematite is used to stimulate the mind; tiger eye is used for focus, grounding, courage, balancing, and optimism (it's an excellent personal power stone for manifesting ideas into reality); aventurine is often used for good fortune and prosperity (as is tiger eye) and helps with self-confidence, stress-relief, motivation, healing, and creativity; rose quartz promotes self- and universal love, forgiveness, compassion, and it's also calming.

You may notice this strand is almost all quartz-based—there's a reason for that. The stones complement each other due to similar properties. The metallic hematite and the silver act as conductors.

After you create the strand, dedicate it. Wait for a waxing moon—ideally, begin with a new moon and complete the dedication at the full moon. Use any format or dedication ritual you choose. I like to place the beads on my altar and, every night, hold them and visualize them being empowered with energy. You may wish to burn a candle near them for a few hours each night.

Someone once said that prayer is speaking to the divine and meditation is listening. While you can use prayer beads as a meditation device, this strand is intended for actual prayer—for sending your thoughts, wishes, desires, and needs into the universe. Visualize your request for guidance, strength, calming—whatever you need.

There's no right or wrong way to use prayer beads. If you're familiar with the Catholic rosary, you know that the number of beads helps one to remember the number of times to say a prayer. For your personal beads, you decide how to use them. For this particular strand, the correspondence with the Fibonacci Sequence is intended to create a harmonious feeling, along with the quartz beads that serve a specific purpose.

The circle is a popular symbol to its never-ending nature, but this set of beads is a strand. In this way, the series of beads comes to an end point and you can imagine a culmination; a sending of your thoughts to the universe.

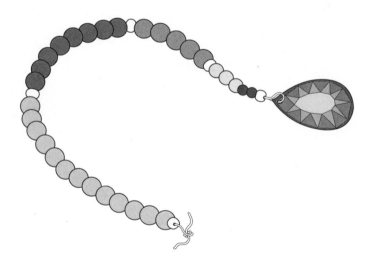

Prayer Beads

To begin using the beads, hold the pendant, focus your mind, and breathe deeply. Visualize your personal soul aligning with the universal spirit. Once you memorize the pattern of beads, you can close your eyes as you use them. You can say your own words or use the chant provided.

Begin by holding the quartz pendant. Focus on calming your mind and spirit, reaching out to the universe, goddess, or any other divine presence. This act establishes your intent. The silver lets you know there's a transition to the next set of beads, hematite. This deepens your focus and sharpens your intent. The three clear quartz beads are designed to carry your thoughts seamlessly to the next stage. Use the two hematite and three quartz beads to visualize your movement from self to reaching out to the divine; next, a silver transition bead. For the five tiger eye beads, consider that five is the number of life. Use these to focus on aspects of your life that you wish to ask for help with, moving to the material aspects represented by the aventurine. And, finally, rose quartz at the end represents the culmination, self- and universal love.

Beginning
Hear my voice, know my heart,
with these words, I impart
all I hope, all I feel
in this prayer, I reveal.

Speak the words for each bead in the series.

2 Hematite
Know my mind, I begin,
seek without; look within.

3 Clear Quartz
In my soul, I reflect,
spirit-world, I connect.

5 TIGER EYE
Focused will, at my best,
all my goals, manifest.

8 AVENTURINE
Health and wealth, fortune mine,
nurture me, flesh and mind.

13 ROSE QUARTZ
Love of self, love to share,
Love divine, everywhere.

If this sounds like more of a spell than a prayer to you, that's probably because they are quite similar. Try to memorize these words so that as you say them, your mind will be free to visualize your specific personal needs and goals. The words will become like a rhythm and you'll know them by heart—the perfect accompaniment to your visualized prayers. The act of memorization can also keep your mind free to embody the words of the chant. Don't try to rush through the prayer as rote memorization—feel the words; know them. Put your desires behind them.

You can recite the chant as you string the beads, if you'd like. Remember, what I've written here is just an example. You can use your knowledge of numerology and stones to create your own personal set of prayer beads.

Crossroads Spell

This spell calls for a "cross-stone"—chiastolite. This special formation is a unique variety of andalusite—crystals of andalusite with cross or "x" shaped inclusions of carbon. It is named for a location where it was once abundant, Andalucia, Spain.

This spell can be used if you're seeking an answer or solution, especially during divination. Cross-stone assists one with change and transitions, death and rebirth, and astral travel. It is an excellent problem-solving stone for use in mediation. It also enhances creativity, practicality, and it can help one maintain spirituality during an illness. It is also useful when one needs to find balance.

Hold the stone, and focus on your question or problem.

CHANT:
I face a crossroads at this time,
Like a mountain I must climb.
I seek an answer or some aid,
Help me not to be afraid.
To make a choice or to decide,
I have the strength I need inside.

You can carry the stone or sleep with it under your pillow or mattress.

Onyx Meditation for Balance

Real onyx can be pure black or banded black and white—a popular myth states that onyx must always be completely black. In fact, black onyx can be created artificially using dye (jewelry stones sold as "black onyx" are often not real quartz onyx). Onyx is similar to agate, but the bands are often straight or in parallel curves in shades of brown and white or black and white; the bands in agate are curved. "Mexican onyx" is actually banded calcite and is often used to create statues and other small carvings. Most onyx sold today is not genuine quartz onyx, so be a careful shopper.

This meditation calls for a piece of real onyx—any color or pattern. A smooth-shaped stone is best, but a piece set in jewelry can also be used. Use this meditation prior to spell work or any time you need general balance. Onyx is good for centering and for opening yourself to trust your instincts, as well.

Prepare as you normally would for meditation. Sit comfortably and hold the onyx in your receptive hand. Visualize the balance of forces in the universe—night and day, the yin and yang—two sides necessary for balance. See them coming together in perfect harmony within you.

CHANT:

Stone of earth against my skin
Balance energy within.
Yin and yang, dark and light—
Let the opposites unite.

Totem Stone Dedication Ritual

Perhaps you have a stone that features the image of one of your totem animals: a stone carved in the animal's shape, or a stone with the animal's image engraved or painted on it. This ritual is for dedicating the stone and for helping you connect with the energy of your totem animal(s).

Like personal power stones, people often have several animal totems for specific purposes or discover that their animal totems change depending on need. Or, you may have a stone carving you wish to use for another purpose even if that creature is not one of your totems. Often the carved shapes are created from a mineral such as quartz, but painted stones are typically ordinary rocks. I have acquired many of these over the years—in an art museum gift shop I found a tiger eye pendant carved in the shape of one of my totems, and on a recent trip to Seattle, I purchased a stone bearing a hand-painted image of another. I have also collected onyx carvings of animals over the years. If you have some of these items, they can be useful magical tools.

To dedicate your stone, create an altar arrangement to honor the animal. Place the stone inside a circle of clear quartz points, points facing toward the stone. You can add candles or incense if you like or other items of personal significance, but be sure to include at least one other representation of your totem animal on the altar, depending on the type of creature. For example, if your totem is a bird, try to incorporate a feather from that specific bird (or any feather if you don't have one from that type). A picture or drawing of the animal is perfectly fine to use, and may be the only other representation you have, especially if the animal is mythical. A statue of the totem animal would also be an excellent choice. Use your imagination and create a space to honor this creature. If you have several totem animals you wish to honor, create a separate dedication for each of them. However, it's perfectly fine to display images of all of them on your regular working altar.

Once your totem altar is assembled, light candles and/or incense as desired and visualize your totem animal. Focus on the creature's characteristics and why this animal is meaningful to you. If you're still in the exploration stage, focus on connecting with this creature and discovering why it has made itself known to you. Use this chant:

> *Creature, you have come to me—please make known the reason.*
> *I seek connection to you now in proper time and season.*
> *Teach me wisdom of your ways, council me throughout the days,*
> *Guide me by your image here with energy I raise.*

You can repeat this ritual any time you like to connect with the totem animal or dedicate any object associated with it. Afterward, you may wish to keep a representation of the animal on your altar at all times or carry its image with you in some way. Wearing a symbol of your totem animal as jewelry is also a good option.

Scrying Spell

While this spell is intended for use with a crystal ball, you can use it for other methods as well. Scrying, which means "to make out dimly," can be done with just about any substance that's translucent or reflective—water, metals, stones, flames, or mirrors. The intent is to clear the mind and look for patterns or images. Don't expect to see pictures—you may see images in your mind, symbols, suggestions—use your intuition to interpret these. When you gaze intently upon a polished surface, eventually, the optic nerve becomes fatigued. Impressions from within the brain are then "seen"—sometimes, if done too long, the nerve actually becomes temporarily paralyzed. Don't attempt scrying for too long without a break, especially if you're new to it.

If you are using a crystal ball, be sure to cleanse, clear, and program or dedicate your sphere as desired. A sphere of real, clear quartz with inclusions (as opposed to a perfectly clear stone) actually works best for crystal ball scrying—the light plays off the inclusions in the stone and can help you visualize. In fact, most real clear quartz spheres are not perfect. I don't recommend using a lead crystal ball—these are glass and not nearly as effective as real stone. You may even want to try obsidian or jet. Your choice of object provides an avenue for your intuition.

Place the crystal or other reflective surface on a table in front of you, so you can sit comfortably and look upon it. To prevent reflections from other objects surrounding you, use a bit of black cloth both under the crystal and behind it—you can drape it over a box to make a backdrop. Darken the room and use candlelight. Place candles in front of the backdrop but behind the crystal—any type of candles will do. Some people like to use tapers (seven is a traditional number), but you can try other sizes and numbers to see what works best for you. Move the candles around until you achieve your desired lighting. Before you begin, use this chant to focus:

Crystal orb, tiny moon,
bring my senses all in tune.
Help me see, more than stone,
help me know, let it show.
Surface shine, as I stare,
Insight true, I'm aware.

Do whatever you can to avoid distractions during the scrying process. Place your hands flat on the table, palms down, or on your lap, palms up. Relax, and don't literally stare into the stone; rather, allow your eyes to go into soft focus, as though you're looking at one of those 3D "magic eye" prints. Try this starting for a few minutes at a time, working up to five minutes. Your eyes may water—if so, stop. Don't try too hard, and take a break if you get tired. Try holding the crystal sphere in your hands for a while, if you'd like—sometimes this helps establish a connection. Don't worry if scrying doesn't work for you, it's not a technique everyone can master right away. Keep practicing.

Pendulums

Crystal pendulums are often used in divination and are believed to work with Earth's natural radiation. Pendulums have been used by ancient civilizations to locate mineral deposits and water (dowsing).

Your inner self has the answer you seek, and the pendulum gives motion to what you already know. It can serve as an outlet for your intuition; some people consider this intuition as coming from a spirit guide or the higher self. The pendulum translates the language into consciousness. Use the pendulum to answer yes or no questions.

Manmade points are best because they're perfectly balanced, but you can try a variety of shapes. These perfectly cut stones can be purchased at metaphysical shops. I like to use clear quartz, but you can try using other types of stone. Suspend the stone from a silver chain—you can purchase stones that are wrapped with wire or set in a pendant style setting; sometimes pendulums are sold with cords, but silver works best in my experience. Practice with your pendulum to determine how it swings to answer a yes or no question.

Some people like to use tarot cards, pictures, or other symbols and hold the pendulum over them while focusing on a question to see if the crystal points to a particular object. Experiment with several of these methods to find one that works for you. Try to leave emotions out of the way. Be open and neutral.

Technique is important: Use a chain or string that is about 5 inches long. Be sure to keep your arm straight—parallel to the surface you're using. Relax your wrist. Use your thumb and index finger to hold the chain—this technique takes practice. After about eight to ten swings you should get a sense of how your pendulum feels. Stop the pendulum, then start again with the neutral swing—this time focus on making the pendulum swing in a specific way—circular or elliptical. Practice with this, eventually making the pendulum swing counterclockwise, clockwise, and even bringing it to a halt.

Next, practice with responses. Ask yes or no questions you're certain of and see how the pendulum moves. After you are certain of your pendulum's motions, you are ready to practice divination with it. You can even dowse with drawings, patterns, and grids to find answers to your questions. You can use a simple list of numbers or a spectrum of colors.

**HERE'S A RITUAL YOU CAN USE TO PROGRAM
AND DEDICATE YOUR PENDULUM:**

Hold the pendulum in your projective hand and visualize your intended use of the pendulum in divination. Use this chant:

*I dedicate this stone
To help me see unknown.
For insight I divine
And wisdom in good time.*

As you use your pendulum for divination, try this chant:

*To and fro,
Answer show.
I appeal—
Now reveal.*

– NINE –

Numerology:
Stones by Number

Introduction

Magicians of antiquity considered the understanding of numbers to be essential to their arts. In magic, numbers have always been considered for calculations, formulas, potions, alchemy, measurement of time, and so on. We use numbers to mark celestial movements, make predictions, and in some ways, know the future. By studying their patterns, we know when certain planets will occupy particular areas of space, and how to determine solstices, equinoxes, alignments, and eclipses.

There are many ways to incorporate numerology into your crystal magic practice. If each number has a specific vibration, discovering these correspondences can help us find balance and create harmonious relationships in our surroundings since food, objects, colors, and people all vibrate.

This is a common New Age belief. Scientific study has not made any claims, but crystal healers often work with these principles in mind since crystals are also said to vibrate to specific numbers. Some numerologists say you should find the numbers missing in your name and work with stones based on those missing numbers. Those missing numbers are calculated using a numerology chart.

Numbers can be translated into letters of names; dates of birth can be used to calculate a person's birth number. And, of course, numbers figure predominantly in the study of astrology and birth charts. Musical intervals and chords produce harmonious and beautiful sounds that people have always responded to. Numbers are associated with various meanings, planets, and characteristics. And, naturally, numbers are an important aspect of crystal structure.

Let's begin by finding numbers that will lead to stones you can work with.

Finding Your Numbers

Somewhat like the practice of astrology, numerology seeks to guide human behavior, relationships, and other aspects of life and personality based on a person's number. This number can be determined in a variety of ways. Names are one way. This system has Greek, Latin, and Hebrew roots—gematria, the "practice of turning words into numbers," and is often used in divination practices and the interpretation of religious texts. Different systems use different charts. There are many numbers you can calculate—the most common are your birth and name numbers.

For your birth number, the idea is to reduce a number to its smallest parts. Look at the following example:

January 20, 1980
1 + 20 + 1980 = 2001
2 + 0 + 0 + 1 = 3
Your birth number is 3.

For your name number, letters are assigned a numerical value—this ancient formula was based on a Hebrew system. These charts allow you to use names to calculate your special number. For example:

By this chart (English translation), Jane Doe's number is 9:

1 + 1 + 5 + 5 + 4 + 6 + 5 = 27
2 + 7 = 9

1	2	3	4	5	6	7	8	9
A	B	C	D	E	F	G	H	I
J	K	L	M	N	O	P	Q	R
S	T	U	V	W	X	Y	Z	

Here's another chart, more closely based on the Hebrew alphabet:

1	2	3	4	5	6	7	8
A	B	C	D	E	U	O	F
I	K	G	M	H	V	Z	P
J	R	L	T	N	W		
Q		S		X			
Y							

By this chart, Jane Doe's number is: 1

1 + 1 + 5 + 5 + 4 + 7 + 5 = 28 = 10
1 + 0 = 1

Try calculating your number with each chart and compare your results. Do you "like" one outcome more than the other? If so, use that one. Or, experiment with both. In Jane Doe's case, having numbers 9 and 1, she could add them for a total of ten, giving her the number 1. You may wish to add both of your numbers and reduce that to discover yet another outcome.

Now that you have some numbers to work with, let's find some corresponding stones.

The subsequent pages contain lists of correspondences for using numbers and stones. First, there is a list of numbers and the stone(s) most commonly associated with each, as well as some folklore on the numbers. Next, you'll find a list of stones that correspond to natal signs; a list of traditional birth stones based on month is also included. The end of this chapter contains some specific spells that incorporate numerology.

The stone correspondences listed here pertain to the numerical influence, not necessarily the planet or sign. Not every number has a stone or metal associated with it; these are the ones most often cited in folklore and magical practice.

Note: the planet and the god or goddess the planet was named for are separate entities. Much of this information comes from sources attributed to Pythagoras, who noted the names of Greek gods and goddesses; some of the planets (which now bear the names of Roman gods) were not known during his time. In addition, folklore associated with the number is also provided.

How to Begin

Start by determining your birth number; this is the most popular numerological association—names are easily changed but you can't change your birthday. This is also a good reason to start by working with stones based on your astrological sign.

Scan the lists in the following pages to find some stones that correspond with your number. For example, my birth number is 8; I'm a Libra, which is associated with the number 6. Diamond and onyx both correspond to 8; diamond is also listed under stones for Libra. Since diamond is common to both, this stone would be a good one for me to start with.

In addition, since Libra's number is 6, opal and copper are good choices for me. Opal is a traditional birth stone for the month of October but I'm a September Libra, so sapphire is also on my list as a traditional birth stone. However, the stone one chooses also depends on the type of spell as well as the access to stones in one's collection. Explore all your options. I don't have any diamonds or sapphires that are not set in jewelry, but I do have raw pieces of opal and copper, which may be my best choices. You can also work with your moon sign, ascendant sign, or other aspects of your natal chart. In this case, if copper or opal didn't correspond with my goals, I would seek other options, such as finding the stone of the day. Or I might decide to pick from the list of natal stones or calculate my name number.

If some information among natal stones, birth stones, and numbers seems contradictory, it's because there are many ways to determine correspondences—some of them overlap, but there are bound to be differences. Some correspondences are calculated based on folklore, elements, or astrology. Others are based on color or associations with gods and goddesses. But this produces a wide range of opportunities so you should always be able to find something you can use. In addition to finding stones that correspond with your name or date of birth, you can use numbers with stones to create your own grids (see chapter ten). And, if you wish, use the ritual in chapter eight to dedicate a personal power stone.

Numerological Associations

The first stones listed that correspond with each number are based on folklore and planetary associations. The second list is the number to which these stones are said to "vibrate." Please note this "vibration" is not a scientific term; it has nothing to do with the movement of subatomic particles. These vibrations are calculations using the stone's name with the number chart. It's the energy associated with the letters (using the

English translation chart in this chapter). You may use the chart to calculate any stone's name; I have simply listed some of them here for your convenience.

ONE (1)—topaz, amber

Stones that vibrate to the number 1: aquamarine, azurite, barite, bronzite, copper, mica, obsidian, turquoise

....

The number of solitude, permanence, unity, roots, beginning, divine spark, self-expression, ambition, and courage; others say it is both male and female, being added to odd makes it even and it makes the even odd. It's the center of the circle (the Sun), willpower, determination, leadership. Pythagoreans called it the monad—always the same, seperate from the multitude. It's also said to represent the mind. The gods Apollo and Jupiter and the goddess Vesta (hearth center) were associated with this number. This number rules the sign of Leo. In a grid, you may consider some of these elements as the center, to represent the Sun, life spark, or the spirit.

TWO (2)—moonstone, silver, pearl, and emerald

Stones that vibrate to the number 2: bornite (peakcock ore), garnet, gypsum, gold, granite, howlite, iron, sapphire, tourmaline

....

Two symbolizes reflection, polarity, duality, balance, harmony of opposites, the unconscious mind, duality of humanity and the divine, emotions, harmony, cooperation, wealth, mystery, money, marriage, feminine energy (the moon) peace, and receptivity. The Pythagoreans considered 2 to be the duad or dyad—divided; the mother, but also separateness; polarity. Two was associated with Isis, Diana, Ceres; the mother figure. Two rules the sign of Cancer. In a grid, use two to represent a harmony of opposites, male and female. Or, you can consider two symbolic of Illusion (like the Moon card in tarot).

THREE (3)—turquoise

Stones that vibrate to the number 3: amber, amethyst, aventurine, chiastolite, dolomite, Herkimer diamond, lapis lazuli, pyrite, ruby
....

Three represents synthesis, movement, divinity, manifestation, trinity, creativity, joy, bridge between sky and earth, expansion, versatility, expressiveness, and luck. Pythagoreans considered this—the triad—to be the first real number. The oracles of Apollo sat upon a tripod, the number being equilibrium; the number of knowledge and wisdom. The musical ratios of 3:2 and 3:1 are intervals of the fifth—the loveliest of harmonies aside from the octave itself. Made up of the monad and duad, the triad was sacred and was associated with the god Saturn, the goddess Hecate, the gods Pluto and Triton, and the three Fates, Furies, and Graces. The number three is ruled by the planet Jupiter and is the number of the sign of Sagittarius. For a grid (see chapter ten), use three for a sacred trinity of any kind—Maiden, Mother, and Crone, for example.

FOUR (4)—sapphire, quartz, and a blend of azurite and malachite

Stones that vibrate to the number 4: apophyllite, bloodstone, chiastolite, emerald, hemimorphite, kyanite, lead, moonstone, rhodochrosite, rutile, rhyolite, silver, sodalite, tiger eye, zircon (A note about tiger eye: You may see it spelled as tiger's eye or tigereye in other sources. According to the *National Audubon Society Field Guide to North American Rocks and Minerals* the name is tiger eye, so that's the spelling I use. In this case, the spelling of a gem name could change its number.)

....

Four is the number of Earth energy, the four classical elements, solidarity, crossroads, discipline, will, order, practicality, endurance, efficiency, materiality, and instinct. The Pythagorean tetrad was the root of all things, the "perfect number." It was order, symbolic of the divine; balanced; the first geometric solid; the soul (consisting of the four powers: mind, science, opinion, and sense). Four was associated with the gods Mercury, Hercules, Vulcan, and Bacchus. (The planet Uranus wasn't known in the times of Pythagoras.). Four is the number of the sign of Aquarius and the planet Uranus. A grid based on four represents stability.

FIVE (5)—aquamarine, platinum, and silver

Stones that vibrate to the number 5: amazonite, carnelian, chrysocolla, peridot

....

Five represents humanity and life itself, protection, love, reproduction, regeneration, strength, intelligence, the five senses, freedom, communication, struggle, confusion, curiosity, adventure, and sensory experiences. Pythagoreans called this the pentad—the union of odd and even, sacred symbol of light, health, and vitality. A perfect division of the perfect number, ten, it also contains the fifth element, ether. Five is symbolic of nature (only 5 and 6 when multiplied by themselves end in their original number). 4 plus 1, the elements plus the monad, equal 5. The pentagram is a sacred symbol of life and associated with the goddess Venus. The planet Venus makes a fivefold pattern as it orbits the sun. We find fives everywhere in nature—even in our physical form. The associated planets are Venus and Mercury; the astrological signs of Gemini and Virgo. Use five in grids for a pentagram shape—one of the oldest magical symbols.

SIX (6)—opal, copper

Stones that vibrate to the number 6: apache tear, bloodstone, citrine, creedite, jade, labradorite, onyx, topaz

....

Six is, like four, a "perfect number" symbolizing beauty, union of conscious and unconscious minds, balance, creation, perfection, wholeness, healing, love, wisdom, responsibility, release, union of opposites, idealism, loyalty, harmony, domesticity, and truthfulness. Pythagoreans called this the hexad, and it was the creation of the world—perfection; the union of two triangles. Six is the sum and product of the first three numbers (1, 2, 3) and its factors are also 1, 2, and 3. This is one reason it's called a "perfect" number. To the Pythagoreans, it symbolized harmony, marriage, and balance (and was associated with Orpheus). Crystalline structures such as snowflakes and quartz crystals are built on the number six, a cube has six sides, and honeycombs are hexagrams. The astrological signs associated with six are Taurus and Libra. The Pythagoreans did not associate a planet/goddess with 6; however, it corresponds to the planet Venus based on the signs of Taurus and Libra. Grids using six represent harmony and perfection, also healing and love.

SEVEN (7)—amethyst, emerald

Stones that vibrate to the number 7: agate, fluorite, iolite, pearl, platinum, sulfur, tin, wulfenite

....

Seven represents perfect order, a mystical and sacred number, higher learning, spirituality, magic, wisdom, law, intelligence, divinity, mystery, and solitude. In Pythagorean philosophy, the heptad was the number of religion and life, fortune, judgment, dreams, and sounds. It was associated with the god Mars. 3 plus 4—soul plus world—equals the mystic nature of man, the three-fold soul or spirit (spirit, mind, and soul). There are seven chakras, seven visible colors in the spectrum, and seven days of the week—named for the seven celestial bodies of ancient times. The Pythagoreans associated this number with the god Mars; seven is also associated with the god Osiris and the planet Neptune (based on its association with the sign of Pisces since the planet Neptune was not known to the Pythagoreans). The number seven has long been regarded as a mystery number among various religious traditions. Grids for wisdom, mystery, and spirituality are the purposes for grids using this number.

EIGHT (8)—diamond, onyx

Stones that vibrate to the number 8: calcite, fossils, jet, lepidolite, mica, opal, marcasite, serpentine
....

Eight is the number of strength, life-force energy, discipline, eternity, authority, courage, regeneration, good luck, justice, practicality, power, salvation or spiritual evolution, karma, balance, and material success. Pythagoreans called this ogdoad and it symbolized love, counsel, and the god Neptune. It was associated with the Eleusinian Mysteries. Eight was special because it could be divided into 4 then 2 and then each 2 separated back to 1. The eighth note on the musical scale is the octave. Eight corresponds to the planet Saturn and the sign of Capricorn. Grids using eight represent strength and courage.

NINE (9)—ruby

Stones that vibrate to the number 9: apatite, aragonite, fuchsite, hematite, malachite, rhodonite, unakite, vanadinite
....

Nine represents completeness, change, achievement, culmination, order, action, physical prowess, forgiveness,

compassion, inspiration, spirituality, and divine love.
Pythagoreans called this ennead; it's the first square of an
odd number: 3 x 3. Nine is the first number that can be used
to construct a magic square. Nine was called the number
of man by the Pythagoreans (human gestation time is nine
months). But, since nine falls short of the perfect number, 10,
it symbolized horizon and boundary to the Pythagoreans. It
gathered all numbers within itself. It was associated with the
god Prometheus and the goddess Juno. The corresponding
planet is Mars and the sign is Aries. Grids using 9 can
represent a wide variety of magical purposes.

....

There is much magic surrounding the number 9. If you add
up the numbers 1–9 it equals 45, and 4 plus 5 is 9. Nine can't
be destroyed no matter how many times you multiply or add
it—and this is true for no other number. All products of nine
can be reduced to nine. Try it: 3 times 9 is 27, and 2 plus 7 is
9. Nine times nine is 81 and 8 plus 1 is nine. Nine times 4 is
36 and 3 plus 6 is 9.

TEN (10)—no specific stone associations

Ten is perfection through completeness, return to unity, transformation,
a plateau. Called the decad, it was the greatest of numbers, the very
nature of numbers; heaven and the world; power, faith, memory;
tireless—associated with Atlas and the sun. We have ten fingers and
ten toes; Plato believed it contained all numbers. Since ten is the
first number with two digits, it's often associated with opposites and
balance.

ZERO (0)—no specific stone associations

Some may argue that zero is not actually a number … throughout
history, various cultures have gone through confusion over
how nothing can be something and whether or not it should

be valued, and how. Zero often represents the universal—everything. Associated with Pluto, rules Scorpio. And yet, zero represents power—think about it: if you keep adding zeros to a number, it grows from 10 to 100 to 100,000. It also represents eternity, the circle, the serpent eating its tail.

Natal Stones

Here is a compiled list of natal stones based on the signs of the Zodiac. This list also includes the ruling planet(s), associated colors, the corresponding number for each sign, and the element. See the Appendix for more stones associated with the planets.

If you study astrology, you know how complex a natal chart can be. For beginners, start with your sun sign, rising sign (ascendant), and moon sign. You probably already know your sun sign. But a person's rising sign can actually be as significant, if not more, than the sun sign. The sign the moon occupies at your time of birth offers yet another layer of characteristics. Think of it this way (this is a very simplistic view, but it will serve): your sun sign is the inner you—the person those closest to you know; your rising sign reflects more of your outward personality; your moon sign reflects your instincts and reactions to what life throws at you. And, each sign is also associated with one of the elements, offering more ways to make use of your personality's various aspects.

If you were born on a cusp (during the moment when the sun changes signs) you may feel like you have two sun signs. Have your chart drawn to find out for sure, based on the exact time and place of your birth; there are many free services online you can use to get a simple natal chart. You may see the influences of two sun signs, but you really do have just one. Most people do exhibit the influence of other signs, especially the ones closest to their sun sign. This may be due to the location of Mercury or Venus. For instance, I'm a Libra, with ascendant also in Libra, but I definitely have some Virgo tendencies—it turns out Mercury was in Virgo when

I was born. Since Mercury and Venus are so close to the sun, it's beneficial to find out where these planets are in your natal chart; knowing their influence can be useful.

So you see, there are many ways to work with natal stones beyond your sun sign. For example, find a stone for your rising sign if you want to enhance your outward characteristics; use your sun sign to find a stone to use for more personal, emotional situations. A stone that corresponds to your moon sign would be useful when you must deal with external issues beyond your control. One way to find an especially strong natal stone is to cross-reference the lists to see if your sun sign, ascendant sign, and moon sign have stones in common.

Aries: amethyst, Apache tear, aquamarine, aventurine, bloodstone, carnelian, citrine, diamond, dolomite, emerald, garnet, gypsum, hematite, iron, jade, jasper, kyanite, ruby
....
Planet/Number/Colors/Element: Mars, 9, crimson, blue, white; Fire

Taurus: agate, aventurine, blue tourmaline, carnelian, chrysocolla, citrine, copper, diamond, emerald, gypsum, iolite, jade, kyanite, malachite, obsidian, rhodochrosite, rhodonite, rose quartz, rutile, tin, zebra rock, zircon
....
Planet/Number/Colors/Element: Venus, 6, rose-pink, blue, brown, green; Earth

Cancer: aventurine, bornite, calcite, carnelian, chrysocolla, emerald, grossular garnet, jade, jasper, moonstone, opal, pearl, peridot, rhodochrosite, ruby, silver, sodalite
....
Planet/Number/Colors/Element: Moon, 2, white, light green, pale yellow, silver, violet, lavender; Water

Gemini: agate (moss), amber, apatite, apophyllite, aquamarine, carnelian, celestite, chrysocolla, citrine, emerald, howlite, jade, lodestone, pearl, rutile, sapphire, serpentine, tiger eye, turquoise, watermelon tourmaline, zebra rock

....

Planet/Number/Colors/Element: Mercury, 5, gray, light green, silver; Air

Leo: amber, black tourmaline, bronzite, carnelian, citrine, diamond, garnet, gold, golden topaz, gypsum, iron, jasper, labradorite, marcasite, onyx, peridot, petrified wood, platinum, pyrite, rhodochrosite, ruby, sulfur, tiger eye, zircon

....

Planet/Number/Colors/Element: Sun, 1, yellow, orange, purple; Fire

Virgo: agate (moss), amazonite, amethyst, azurite, carnelian, chrysocolla, citrine, creedite, fossil, garnet, hematite, jade, jasper, lapis lazuli, lodestone, opal, peridot, ruby, sapphire, sodalite, tiger eye, vanadinite, watermelon tourmaline, zircon

....

Planet/Number/Colors/Element: Mercury, 5, gray, silver, dark green, white; Earth

Libra: apophyllite, aquamarine, bloodstone, carnelian, chiastolite, chrysocolla, citrine, diamond, granite, hemimorphite, iolite, jade, kyanite, lepidolite, malachite, moonstone, obisidan, opal, rose quartz, sapphire, star sapphire, smoky quartz, tin, tourmaline, turquoise

....

Planet/Number/Colors/Element: Venus, 6, rose pink, pastels, light blue; Air

Scorpio: agate, amazonite, fluorite, garnet, hematite, jade, labradorite, malachite, moonstone, obsidian, opal, peridot, rhodochrosite, ruby, topaz, turquoise, unakite

....

Planets/Number/Colors/Element: Pluto, Mars, 0, black, blood red, burgundy, wine, maroon; Water

Sagittarius: amethyst, apatite, aventurine, azurite, black sapphire, blue zircon, copper, Herkimer diamond, iolite, labradorite, lapis lazuli, moonstone, obsidian, opal, peridot, rhyolite, rose quartz, ruby, sapphire, smoky quartz, snowflake obsidian, sodalite, star sapphire, tin, topaz, tourmaline, turquoise, wulfenite

....

Planet/Number/Colors/Element: Jupiter, 3, autumn colors, turquoise, purple; Fire

Capricorn: agate, amethyst, aragonite, black tourmaline, citrine, diamond, fluorite, galena, garnet, jasper, jet, malachite, obsidian, onyx, sapphire, smoky quartz, star sapphire, tiger eye

....

Planet/Number/Colors/Element: Saturn, 8, indigo, navy, brown, dark green; Earth

Aquarius: amazonite, amber, amethyst, aquamarine, barite, blue topaz, blue tourmaline, diamond, fluorite, fuchsite, garnet, hematite, jade, labradorite, malachite, mica, moonstone, onyx, opal, silver, tiger eye (blue), turquoise

....

Planets/Number/Colors/Element: Uranus, Saturn, 4, bright blue, silver, gray, green; Air

Pisces: agate (blue lace), amethyst, aquamarine, bloodstone, carnelian, citrine, diamond, fluorite, garnet, jade, opal, rose quartz, sapphire, turquoise

....

Planets/Number/Colors/Element: Neptune, Jupiter, 7, emerald green, light yellow, pink, white; Water

Traditional Birthstones

This is the list of traditional birthstones commonly used today. This list has evolved over the years and some say has its origins in the biblical Breastplate of the High Priest. In modern times, jewelers have made adaptations to the list.

- **January:** garnet

- **February:** amethyst

- **March:** aquamarine

- **April:** diamond

- **May:** emerald

- **June:** pearl

- **July:** ruby

- **August:** peridot/olivine

- **September:** sapphire

- **October:** opal

- **November:** citrine or gold topaz

- **December:** turquoise or blue zircon

Using Your Numbers in Spells and Rituals

After you find stones that resonate with you based on numbers, there are endless ways to use them. Basically, based on the charts, you can reduce any word or a large number to a single digit and find a corresponding stone. Of course, one can become carried away by all this, allowing life to be ruled by numbers. Use moderation and have fun—don't become obsessed with the numbers. It's simply one more way to seek a harmonious balance in your magical life—not a rule to live by. All kinds of "coincidental" numbers occur in the cosmos. Entire books exist on these subjects, offering endless ways of speculating about cosmic messages, patterns, and meanings. However you look at it, there is much harmony to be found.

Simple Spells

Here are some quick and easy ways to use numerology and stones:

STONE OF THE DAY

Take the current date and reduce it to its smallest number. For example: March 1, 2014

$$3 + 1 + 2 + 0 + 1 + 4 = 11 = 2$$

Check the list for correspondences of the number 2. Wear or carry that stone for the day.

BIRTHDAY STONE

Reduce your age to the smallest number, select a stone. Dedicate the stone on your birthday and wear or carry the stone for an entire year.

YEAR STONE

Reduce the current year to a single number (for example, 2013=6). Dedicate the stone on New Year's Day and wear or carry it for the year

RELATIONSHIP STONES

Find stones for you and a mate, friend, or family member—even a pet. Use date of birth or name. Use these stones in spells or rituals.

ADDRESS STONE

Reduce the street number of your home and select a stone or stones. You can include the street name if you wish, or just use the number. Use these stones for home protection spells or home blessing rituals.

Job Seeker's Spell

When you're seeking employment or have an interview on the horizon, use this spell to enhance your opportunity. There are two versions—one for a waning moon and one for waxing, since we can't determine when the opportunity will arise. Check the moon sign as well to be sure it's conducive to the type of spell. You may want to wait a few days for the best moon sign.

- Determine the birth number. Using the birth number and natal sign, if you wish, select an appropriate stone to represent you (or the seeker, if you're performing the spell for someone else—be sure to obtain that person's consent).

- A white candle (all-purpose) or a yellow or orange candle (success)

- A piece of devil's shoestring (root from viburnum family of shrubs)

- A piece of wulfenite (optional, to increase magical potency)

- A double-terminated quartz point with inclusions of tourmaline (optional, to aid the flow of energy and dispel negativity; creates a "solving atmosphere")

- A strand of the job seeker's hair or a fingernail clipping may be placed under the candle holder, if desired. You may also place the job advertisement under the candle holder or a print of the company's logo.

Arrange the stones and strand of devil's shoestring around the candle. Visualize the desired outcome, light the candle, and chant.

WANING MOON OPTION:
Earth to nurture and to ground,
Fire transform, no longer bound.
Problems of the past resolved—
Fresh new start, be absolved.

WAXING MOON OPTION:
Elements of Earth and Fire
Good employment's my (or name) desire.
Forge a new foundation strong,
Find the place where I (name) belong(s).

AFTER AN INTERVIEW:
Elements of Earth and Fire
This new job is my (name's) desire.
Forge a new foundation strong,
This place could be where I belong (name belongs).

After the candle burns out, allow all objects to remain on the altar until you or the intended person receives more news. You can combine these spells if you'd like, performing each during the appropriate moon phase.

Spell for a Favorable Outcome

This is a general spell you can use for just about anything you need. The key is using stones based on numerology. Here's an example: Let's say you're seeking bids for a project in your home. Reduce your house number, find the corresponding stone, and place the stone in the location (or as near as possible) where the work is needed.

You can also use your personal power stone for this spell. You may choose how to use the stone—wear it, carry it, combine it with candle magic, etc. Hold the stone as you visualize your desired outcome and chant:

I need things to go my way,
Decision in my favor—
Bring good fortune on this day,
An outcome I will savor.

State your goal. Place the stone.

- TEN -

CRYSTAL GRID SPELLS: ADVANCED CRYSTAL MAGIC

Introduction

One of the most basic concepts to grasp when working with crystal magic is that numbers are at the core. As you read in the last chapter, there is harmony in numbers—something that the mystics and scholars of ancient times recognized and explored in their quest to understand how our world works. Crystal structure is based on patterns and numbers; spells based on grids of stones use these numbers for a specific purpose, in addition to many other correspondences based on numbers and geometric shapes.

Geometry means "earth measure," and it was one of the first areas of mathematical study. Such knowledge has always been needed for building structures, measuring land, and other basics of civilized life. Studies of geometry began with simple shapes such as the square, rectangle, circle, and triangle.

Sacred geometry is a study based on the recognition and awareness of certain patterns humans have used for centuries and which seem to occur again and again in what we make, and what we observe in nature and the universe. These patterns reveal our interconnectedness with all things and give us a glimpse into underlying systems. We're part of a magnificent harmonious structure—the mind, our bodies, and our cosmos. Such patterns are a map of the sacred in the scientific. Some say it's the key to understanding life itself—if not the key, at least a doorway.

Much of crystal magic is based on order and symmetry, geometry and numbers. For example, you may be familiar with the Golden Ratio (or Golden Rectangle) and the Fibonacci Sequence. Shapes are of primary importance, especially when working with grids, since they speak to us on a universal level—they are the geometry found in nature, in what we create, and in us. Crystal grids are a form of magic that involves arranging stones in a particular pattern based on a variety of correspondences that can include number, metaphysical and scientific properties of the stone, symbolism of shape, and so on.

Many grids in this chapter use clear quartz points as foundation stones. This is because of their special structure and their function in the spell. Don't worry if your quartz points aren't perfect, they don't have to be. They are used to direct energy as you focus your intent and build the grid. Generally, try to use quartz points that are relatively uniform in size for a grid. This helps preserve the balance and symmetry of the layout. In addition, you may wish to incorporate quartz points with special properties (refer to chapter seven).

The act of setting the stones in place serves a purpose—it's meditative, is intended to help your mind reach a relaxed and meditative state and to help you focus your intent on the task. This is one reason there are often chants to accompany the placement of each stone. The overall shape, stones used, words, and placement all work together to help you focus your intent.

The foundation for your grid is important, especially if you want to keep it in place for a long period of time. Ideally, use a table or altar; make sure you have a stable setting. You can use a board, a piece of cardboard or a tray, if you'd like, in case you need to move the grid. Large plates or serving platters work well too, as do mirrors (you may wish to cover the surface of a mirror with a sheer cloth or veil to avoid scratching it). Of course, the size of the stones you're using will determine your foundation. Don't forget that you can even construct large grids outside and hold rituals inside them.

Diagrams are provided for these spells to help you create the desired shape. In many cases, you can simply arrange the stones in the appropriate pattern. Of course, feel free to place your stones on an outline if you like. You can use paper or a bed of sand (dry or damp), to draw outlines of the shape before adding the stones. The Flower of Life spell is the only one that requires the printed diagram to be used.

An explanation of crystal systems can be found in the Appendix.

Grid for Debt Relief

Use this spell as you begin to take steps toward paying a debt or trying to solve a difficult financial problem. Sometimes a solution can be found by achieving a low interest rate for repaying a debt, finding a consolidation program, or extending payments over a longer period of time. This spell is intended to help clear the way to finding your best strategy. Work diligently toward a resolution and visualize this spell helping you reach your goal.

Perform this spell during a waning moon, when it is in Taurus (stability, money issues), Capricorn (business, money, obligations, stability), or Virgo (practicality and success), if possible.

Stones: aragonite, citrine quartz, fuchsite, grossular garnet, howlite, iolite, malachite, petrified wood, quartz with tourmaline, and vanadinate. There are specific words to recite as each stone is placed.

Adorn your altar with a black cloth and place a copy of a financial statement or bill on top of it—you will build the grid on top of the paper. Start in the upper left corner. As you place each stone on top of the paper, visualize crushing the debt, decreasing it, eliminating it. Say the phrase listed for each stone as you set the stone on the paper, moving counterclockwise, arranging them in a square—four anchor stones, one for each corner, with a total of three across the top and bottom, and four on each side. After all the stones are in place, recite the final chant.

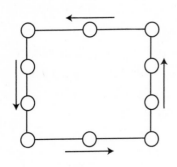

Grid for Debt Relief

Chants:

- tourmalinated quartz: *create the atmosphere to solve this problem*

- howlite: *open the necessary channels of communication, direct my action to this goal*

- malachite: *clear the path for resolution*

- aragonite: *help me to accept responsibility for my debt*

- fuchsite: *help me bounce back from this and be balanced*

- citrine: *grant me financial success*

- vanadinate: *bring order to this process*

- petrified wood: *grant me support in my time of need*

- grossular garnet: *grant me success in this matter*

- iolite: *help me eliminate this debt*

Stones that number ten
This struggle I shall win.
With harm to none please aid
This debt that I have made.
I learned from this event
Forgive what has been spent.

Raise energy as desired. You may wish to burn a black candle in the center of your stone grid. Leave this grid in place until the moon begins to wax. Repeat as desired during each waning moon phase in an appropriate moon sign.

Note: if you have a piece of jewelry that contains one (or more) of the stones listed here, feel free to use it in the spell (rest it on top of one of the stones), and then wear it. Visualize that piece being dedicated to this goal, carrying the spell's momentum with you. A ring or bracelet is ideal, since it will give you a frequent, visual reminder of your goal.

Grid for Peace and Quiet

Have you ever been in a situation out of your control where others were affecting your well-being, disturbing your peace, and you couldn't do anything about it? While we can't control others, we may be able to influence our environment to have the atmosphere we seek. Sometimes people are rude and don't even realize it. And sometimes we are simply stuck in an environment that we can't control. In the case of the latter, we can only hope to influence things in a positive way. This spell falls under the realm of communication, ruled by the element of Air, so we'll use the Air symbol.

STONES:

You will need enough clear quartz points to form a triangle shape.

IN ADDITION:

- **amazonite** (eliminates aggravation) top

- **bronzite** (for courtesy) lower left

- **fossil** (for quality environment) lower right

- **optional:** hemimorphite (to relieve hostility)

Arrange the stones in an upward pointing triangle as indicated in the drawing. The Air symbol has a line across the top; if you have enough quartz points, place stones in this area to form a line. See drawing for stone placement. If using the hemimorphite, place it in the space at the top of the triangle.

Begin at the lower right corner and place the stones working clockwise. Place the hemimorphite last. Visualize energy flowing through the points and stones, outward into your environment. Imagine air flowing and rippling outward around you, sweeping a peaceful atmosphere throughout your surroundings.

After all the stones are in place, chant:

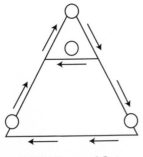

Peaceful let this place now be
Filled with just serenity.
Now let no disruption be
Disturbing to my reverie

Grid for Peace and Quiet

Those that are annoying me
May they cease their task.
I think it's only fair
This favor that I ask.

VARIATION: BANISHING GRID

If the situation is more than just annoying, make a slight change to the grid as follows. Begin in the lower left corner and work your way around counterclockwise.

STONES:

- **hematite** (to transform negativity)

- **bornite** (protection and happiness)

- **black tourmaline** (protection from negative energy)

Place these in any of the three positions and chant:

Get thee now away from me
Far from this vicinity
No more noise or bother be
Get thee now away from me
Your presence here it does me harm
So for good I cast this charm:
Bring forth the peace and calm I seek
As I will so shall it be.

Prosperity Grid

For prosperity we use a simple square—it represents order, balance, stability, the earth and four elements, nurturing, wealth, abundance, and perfection. Perform this spell when the moon is waxing to full, in Taurus, Cancer, or Capricorn if possible.

STONES:

- 8 clear quartz points

- 4 other stones, any combination of pyrite, aventurine, tiger eye, or agate. (Pyrite, tiger eye, and aventurine are the best choices.) You may use all four of the same stone if you wish. Pyrite is good for practicality and keeping a positive outlook; tiger eye is a traditional stone for wealth and money, as well as optimism; aventurine is used for prosperity and is a traditional gambler's stone for good luck. It also helps relieve stress.

Depending on the size of your stones, you may need to form a larger or smaller square. Simply form the square wit your stones on your desired surface. Allow this grid to stay in place for an entire moon cycle, or longer, if desired. Or, if using a candle, you can remove the grid after the candle has burned out. If you are adding this grid to a candle spell of your own, do your candle spell first, then build the grid around it.

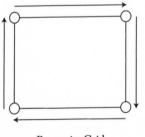

Prosperity Grid

Before you build the stone border, visualize this square as a symbol of your financial situation. This square will be built to protect your assets, and help them grow and remain stable. In the center of the square, either use a symbol or write your need (on the paper or on a separate sheet). You can use a green candle carved with a dollar sign, you can write "paid" on a bill and put that in the center, or simply write "wealth" in the center of the square.

Next, you will build the borders of the square. Begin with one of the other stones in the upper left corner. The quartz points will be placed in between the corner stones with the point following the direction of movement (right on top, then down, then to the left, then up). Work your way around the square, moving clockwise, placing one of the other stones at each corner and then two quartz points. Say this as you place each stone:

Prosperity, wealth to me.

When finished, say this twice:

Fire, Water, Earth, and Air,
With my money do take care.

Grid for Fertility

This spell can be for any endeavor you need to help "grow." It can be for actual fertility for yourself or another, or to help a project grow. This grid uses the elemental Earth symbol and a circle to represent the womb. Trace or draw this symbol on a sheet of paper or in sand.

STONES:
- copper, associated with Venus, adds an elemental representation of Water

- gypsum, for fertility (use its selenite rose formation)

- aventurine, for balance, good fortune, and opportunity

- peridot, Venus, Earth element, regulates cycles

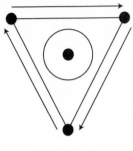

Grid for Fertility

Place the selenite rose in the center of the circle; the other three stones at the points. Move in a clockwise manner, beginning in the upper left corner. After building the grid, chant:

May the seed be planted in the womb,
Let it firmly hold and strongly root.
Let the need I foster grow and bloom
Nourish my desire, bearing fruit.

If that chant is too "birth-like" for your need, here's an alternative:

May the seed in fertile soil land
Let my goal take root and firmly stand.
Give my project ample room to grow
May I harvest richly what I sow.

The Flower of Life Spell

This spell has nothing to do with flowers; it's based on an ancient symbol called the Flower of Life. This symbol is important in sacred geometry for many reasons. It has been identified as representing tones and half tones in music, the pattern of cell division, and a pattern of six "petals" or "star points" around a center—six around one being a common theme in creation myths in many cultures. Some say it's the symbol representing the origin of life. One of the oldest known occurrences of this symbol has been found at the Temple of Osiris at Abydos in Egypt, and images even older are currently being investigated.

Many different forms can be found in the Flower of Life—the seed of life, fruit of life, tree of life, various forms of intersecting circles, and other shapes used for mystical practices. Whatever meaning you ascribe to this symbol, one thing is certain: it's been around for a long time and seems to resonate with people of many cultures. Its symmetry and harmony can't be denied.

For our purpose, this symbol provides a framework for a spiritually enlightening spell or ritual. Seek the connectedness of all things and your place in the universe—the mystery of life itself. However you choose to engage it, this symbol can provide a doorway. You may use the symbol printed here or create your own using a compass. This is just a series of circles that grows increasingly complex, yet we can still see the simplicity. This spell represents balance in all ways of life.

The full image consists of nineteen complete circles. The center of each circle will be a point for a stone to be placed. This will create a geometric pattern of eighteen outer stones with one in the center, for a total of nineteen stones. The numbers 18 and 19 are associated with the sun and moon. Lunar and solar eclipses repeat after eighteen years, full moon dates repeat after nineteen years. It's also interesting to note that there are nineteen stones in the inner structure of Stonehenge. In tarot, the eighteenth card of the major arcana is the Moon, and 19 is the Sun. You will need nineteen small stones, tumbled or raw. You can use various combinations of stones.

STONES:

- For the center, a piece of pyrite can be used to represent the sun, fire, spark of life. You could also use gold, a diamond, or a piece of sunstone . An extraordinarily clear quartz point, such as a Herkimer diamond, would also be a good choice.

- 6 moonstones, for the inner circle of six points

- 12 clear or milky quartz stones (or a combination), for the outer circle of twelve points

You can use a different stone for each "ring" depending on what you have in your collection. It's nice to start with pyrite, then use moonstone, then quartz. This represents the spark of life from the sun, then the moon, then the earth. Alternately, if you don't have these combinations, use whatever you have to represent the sun, moon, and earth. Of course, you can use this model to come up with your own ideas. Remember, this is just a guide to get you started. You can do this alone or with a group, taking turns adding stones.

Whatever method you choose, it's your focus that's important. Start from the center point and add stones to each point radiating outward; moving clockwise may appeal to you.

Think of the connections that make life possible for us—we need the sun and moon. Think of them as balancing us as we live here on earth. We need the sun for life and the moon is important too—there is a theory that when the moon formed it actually hit the Earth and gave us our tilt and important cycles of seasons. It regulates the tides, and is the basis for many of our monthly cycles and measurements. And it symbolizes mystery, intuition, and dreams. We need the balance of day and night, yin and yang. Think of the very beginning of life. Imagine the universe and its mysteries. Ponder the deepest thoughts you can about origins and connections, here on Earth, in the universe, and spiritually. This spell asks us to consider our lives and to be mindful of our actions. Make this spell meaningful to you in whatever way you choose.

Chant as you place each stone:

CENTER:
Honor the beginning, the source that we all share,
Honor all of life, treat everything with care.

CIRCLE OF SIX, ROTATING CLOCKWISE:
Mysteries of life unfold,
Myths and stories yet untold.

Circles, cycles, all connect,
For all of life I have respect.

Enlighten me with the unknown,
Sun and moon your light has shone.

Thank you for the life I/we know
In tune with spirit, let me/us glow.

In the balance, let this flower
Remind me/us daily of my/our power.

In my/our life/lives let me/us instill
love and action with goodwill.

FOR THE OUTER CIRCLE OF TWELVE:
As above, so below—
give me/us light, I/we will grow.

Flower of Life

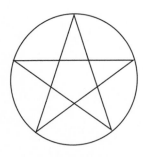

Pentacle Grid

Pentacle Grid

If you have space, you may wish to try this layout in place of a magic circle during spell work or ritual. The pentagram is such a magically potent symbol and, since it's associated with the number 5, it has even further cosmic significance. You can also use this grid for a protection spell—place a photo of the person in need of protection in the center of the grid.

STONES:

- Ten clear quartz points. You can construct this grid on a large enough scale to stand in the center, or make a small one on your altar (you can use a plate or tray, if you'd like).

- Salt

Draw the pentacle in salt. At the five outer points, place the crystals pointing outward. At the five inner points, place the crystals pointing inward. After the stones are in place, use whatever visualization technique you prefer, and chant:

Sending out, drawing in,
Five and five, crystals ten.
Energy, flowing fast—
Aid the spell that I cast.

Add this chant if performing the spell for protection:

Salt and stone, now surround,
In this shape, safe and sound.

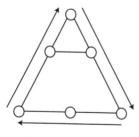

Stimulate the Mind

Spell to Stimulate the Mind

Use this spell for study, creativity, or whenever you need a boost of intellectual focus. This spell uses the elemental Air symbol and the number 6 for balance. Draw or trace the grid onto a sheet of paper or use a bed of sand. Using the stones, start at the bottom right and work your way around, clockwise, placing them where indicated. The order of stones doesn't matter.

STONES:

- **hematite:** "stone of the mind"

- **fluorite:** clear or blend of colors—the "genius stone"

- **calcite:** stimulates memory; good for studying

- **kyanite:** promotes creativity

- **vanadinite:** bridges thought and intelligence

- **tiger eye:** focus and understanding

After the stones are in place, visualize as you choose, and chant:

Let the air move my mind
Take me where I can find
What I need to succeed—
With great care, take me there.

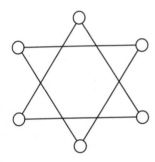

Six-Pointed Star

Sixth Sense Grid

This spell also uses the six-pointed star shape. In this case, use the grid to help boost your sixth sense—psychic awareness.

STONES:

Draw or trace the star pattern on paper or in sand; choose a stone for each sense and position them on the grid as directed as follows; these are recommended for their correspondences with the senses that govern the chakras:

- **smell:** bloodstone, hematite, carnelian, red jasper (bottom point)

- **taste:** rutiliated quartz, tiger eye (bottom left)

- **eyesight:** citrine, amber (bottom right)

- **touch:** aventurine, rose quartz, watermelon tourmaline (top left)

- **sound:** aquamarine, lapis lazuli, turquoise, celestite (top right)

- **sixth sense/third eye:** amethyst, purple fluorite, azurite (top)

- **Optional:** clear quartz or Herkimer diamond in the center.

Visualize the stones representing your senses. Imagine each of them— what aromas do you enjoy? What are your favorite tastes, sights, and sounds? What do you find pleasing to the touch? Work your way up to your sense of intuition. Imagine yourself being aware and in touch with this sense. See yourself balanced like this star, complete and whole, your sixth sense part of your life, guiding you. When you're ready, chant as indicated. If it helps, hold one of the sixth sense stones in your hand while you meditate.

Smell and taste, sight and sound;
touching objects all around.
Intuition and insight—
Senses all, now unite.

Alchemical Grids

Alchemy was part science, part myth, and part spiritual practice—a complex set of philosophies that evolved and changed over time and location. One tradition involved the pursuit of a mysterious substance referred to as the philosopher's stone—a cure-all; it would turn "imperfect" elements into the noble elements like silver and gold, heal the body, and purify the soul. The alchemists saw this as a natural process that only needed to be identified and discovered. Transformation could be seen happening in the natural world constantly—minerals in the earth, such as dirt and rock, would yield fruit on vines and trees, for example. And in our bodies, we break food down into chemicals we need to live. *Transmutation* is the word used to describe the change of one form of matter to another. This change can be both physical and spiritual, which is why alchemy can be viewed as both scientific and allegorical. For magical practice, we turn to the metaphor of change the practice of alchemy has inspired—we seek to create change in ourselves and our world.

The ancient Greeks professed that the entire universe was formed from what we now call the four classical elements (Earth, Air, Fire, and Water), substances (in Western alchemy) that represent the qualities of hot, wet, dry, and cold—the characteristics of which all matter is made (not literally those substances). Earth was heaviest, and located at the center; then Water; next Air, then Fire, lightest and purest of the elements—closest to the divine. This was the ideal state and order of things—the sun (gold) was the purest form. Aristotle referred to the fifth element (ether) as "quintessence"—it was found among the heavens and stars, which were purer than earthly materials. Alchemists sought to bring this fifth element down through transmutation.

The themes of these four grids are drawn from alchemical metaphors, elements, and symbols.

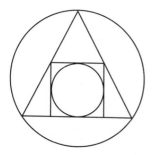

Squaring the Circle

Squaring the Circle

On the left is a seventeenth-century alchemical symbol representing the philosopher's stone.

The human body has often been compared to the larger world and the universe—as above, so below. Psychologist Carl Jung compares the Western idea of the philosopher's stone to the experience of self-realization, or individuation. Profound personal change, like the change of substances, takes time. And so, magically, we explore the use of stones that reveal this change.

A circle or sphere has been used to symbolize the heavens throughout history, while a square or cube has been used to represent the earth. The union of these is a way to symbolically unite heaven and earth, or spirit and matter.

The concept of "squaring of the circle" is a supposedly impossible mathematical formula creating a square shape with the same area as a circle (using only a compass and straight edge). Some scholars in the past came close to solving it (Archimedes, for one), but the solution remains imperfect due to the transcendental nature of the number pi. It has also been used to symbolize the elusive philosopher's stone. We can use this symbol as a metaphor in a spell to deal with a seemingly impossible problem.

The circle is often used to represent the self (the psyche). In addition, circles also symbolize the world and the entire cosmos—continuity and connectedness. In this case, the inner circle is the self and the outer is the cosmos. Surrounding the inner circle is first a square, then a triangle. The square can be used to represent the physical earth, reality. In alchemy, the triangle is the symbol for the element of Fire. The triangle also represents the trinity of mind, body, and spirit. We can then use this symbol to represent the self, on the earth, with the fire of creativity and the trinity, reaching out to the universe. This is how you can approach a challenge. Find a practical way to deal with it, then move toward a creative response and send this intent out to the cosmos. Draw the shape on paper or a bed of sand.

STONES:

Place a stone (or other object that represents you or the issue) in the center of the circle. Recommended stones for the center are Herkimer diamond, amethyst, or your personal power stone.

At the three points of the triangle, use three clear quartz points, pointed outward.

In the spaces marked with an X, use six stones from this list:

- **tourmalinated quartz:** problem solving
- **creedite:** removes obstacles, spiritual clarity
- **apatite:** insight and clarity
- **hematite:** mental processes
- **bloodstone:** enhances decision making
- **yellow fluorite:** order, intellect, and creativity
- **onyx:** centering, instinct, decision-making
- **rhyolite:** resolution

After all the stones are in place, meditate on the issue or problem. Allow your mind to expand.

CHANT:

The lock is lost, a paradox, enigmas wrapped
inside a box. Find the key, the mystery—solve the puzzle

haunting me. Issues begging for resolve,
riddles that I need to solve; illusions capture—
solutions fail, ideas lurk behind the veil. Open
and reveal to me—distill solution, glean from thee.

Becoming Gold—Your Best Self

Like Squaring the Circle, this spell also uses the analogy of alchemy as a metaphor for perfecting the self. No matter what your future goals are, or where you currently stand in reaching them, strive to live to your highest good and potential each day. The present is all we really have. This spell draws on the journey from Saturn to the Sun, a spiritual journey of the soul from lead to gold.

One way to utilize this spell is to meditate for guidance in discovering your true desire. Visualize yourself climbing up a pyramid, even if you don't know what awaits at the top. If you do have a plan, personally or professionally, visualize your goal at the top and see yourself ascending, reaching it. On a spiritual level, you can simply use this spell any time you feel lost or confused, or whenever you just need a boost of spiritual energy; a chance to reboot yourself. If you ever feel like you've gone off track or you sense you aren't living up to your potential, use this spell to realign yourself with your purpose and goals. It can be as simple as a desire to be your best—living a healthy lifestyle, perhaps, or helping others.

Ultimately, the process of alchemy concerns transformation. This practice can best be explained by imagining that the alchemist, in order to spiritually heal the world (and himself), must find a way to get through the seven spheres of the cosmos and reach spiritual gold. This journey begins with Saturn/lead and moves through these stages: Jupiter/tin, Mars/iron, Venus/copper, Mercury/quicksilver, Moon/silver, and finally, to the Sun/gold. Gold was considered to be perfection.

STONES:

You will need the following stones or metals, associated with the planets:

- **Saturn:** lead, galena, or vanadinite

- **Jupiter:** tin or pewter (amethyst or lepidolite may be used as substitutes)

- **Mars:** iron, pyrite, or hematite

- **Venus:** copper (or a mineral containing copper such as malachite, azurite, or bornite)

- **Mercury:** Since we can't get our hands on the real (and toxic) mercury, use aventurine quartz or a piece of mica.

- **Moon:** Silver (use a piece of sterling silver jewelry)

- **Sun:** Gold (use a piece of gold jewelry, at least 10k)

Since most of us don't have nuggets of metal lying around, you can use jewelry if necessary. For example, when I need pewter I either use pewter jewelry or a statue. In addition, if you have a special gold pendant or ring, it would be appropriate to wear it as a symbol representing this spell's goal.

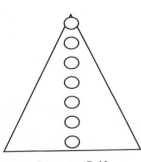

Becoming Gold

You can draw this grid on paper or create it on a bed of sand. Build this grid by adding stones from bottom to top, placing each stone/metal in its appropriate place. As you place each object, visualize a journey. Say the first four lines before you begin; for each of the seven stones there are two lines to chant (and, in keeping with the numerology of 7, each line has seven syllables).

As I reach toward the sun
On this journey I've begun.
Start with lead and turn to gold

Like the alchemists of old.
From this base I find my way

Seeking more and more each day.
With each step my body grows

With each thought my mind it knows
Saving iron from the rust

In myself I learn to trust.
In my soul I learn to shine

Love and light will intertwine.
In myself I see the light

My goals and dreams I will hold tight.
Like the moon your light I share

One more step will take me there.
Spirit rising turns to gold

Highest self I now behold.

Grid for Universal Love

Another symbol with a long history in various religious and occult traditions is the six-pointed star, a hexagram, also called the Seal of Solomon and the Star of David. A powerful magical symbol, it can be used to unite the alchemical symbols for Fire and Water. When the two are joined in the star shape, Earth and Air are symbolized as well– thus, the elements are united. This union of the four elements is another symbol of the philosopher's stone—the fifth element. This grid also gives us the beautiful balance of the number six.

Use this grid to seek universal love and harmony in your life. You can also use this to promote intuition— you open your mind to insight by finding internal harmony.

STONES:

- **Option 1**: Use six clear quartz points

- **Option 2**: Any six of the following stones that have a trigonal structure: rose quartz (universal love), smoky quartz (balancing), amethyst (calming and balancing), sapphire (peace and joy), agate (general good health), calcite (healing) hematite (balancing, grounding, purifying), bloodstone (balancing and purifying), and rhodochrosite (love and balance)

- **Option 3**: Use a combination of clear quartz points and any of the following stones that have a hexagonal internal structure: aquamarine (psychic ability), emerald (love and harmony), apatite (insight/clarity), vanadinite (mental processes and meditation)

Draw the star on a piece of paper (or in sand) and place the stones on the six points.

Visualize yourself as being in harmony with the universe and con- nected to all things. Quiet the chaos of your thoughts. Be still. You are open to all loving relationships; you are surrounded by beauty.

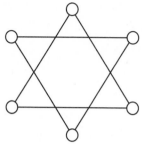

Six-Pointed Star

CHANT:

Balance, center, calming,
I am now becoming
One who knows the meaning—
Hear the silence singing.
Harmony and glory,
Happiness surrounds me.
I possess the beauty,
Love has finally found me.

Each line has six syllables—repeat the entire chant six times.

Spiral Spell for Change

Sulfur was commonly used in alchemy, and since alchemy can be used as a metaphor for change, sulfur is used in this spell. Sulfur is a lovely bright yellow crystal and it's quite soft, so handle your specimen with care. And remember, it's toxic, so wash your hands after working with it.

This spell calls for change when you feel stagnant or for transformation when you're ready for a new phase of your life. Remember: the change could be sudden. Perform this spell on a Thursday, any moon phase or sign.

STONES:

- **barite rose**: all things are possible

- **agate** (your choice of color): for personal development

- **petrified wood**: to change what you can

- **lodestone**: for guidance

- **lepidolite**: stone of transition, to ease the change

- **sulfur**: to facilitate change and transformation

- **hematite:** stone of the mind and of transformation

- **gypsum:** (satin spar), ends stagnation

- **amethyst:** often used for spiritual needs and transformation

For this grid, we will use a spiral shape, symbolic of growth and change. Beginning in the center, work your way around the spiral placing the stones in any order. You can create the spiral on any surface, but a bed of sand is an excellent choice for building this grid. You can draw a spiral first and then add the stones. Use one line of the chant for each stone.

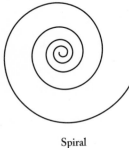

Spiral

Circle, spiral, moving on,
Spinning, changing, look beyond.
See potential meant for me,
Promise, opportunity.
Current state cannot remain
The only constant state is change.
What I need, what's meant for me,
For good of all
So shall it be.

Conclusion

Consider This

Do crystals hold the secrets of the universe? Do they keep a historical record of time? In some ways, yes. Geologically, they tell the story of our earth, and even our universe. This is why a serious crystal enthusiast will study all aspects of geology as well as metaphysical properties of stones.

Stones, like other magical tools, are designed for focus. So why, you say, if our minds have all the power, do we have lists of metaphysical properties of certain stones? Because due to their structure, color, mineral content, location, or other characteristics, some stones are better suited for certain tasks, based on our human perception of them. These attributes were given to the stones by people over time and they resonate with us. Just like various colors, scents, and sounds can affect our mood and state of mind, certain stones can do this as well. We are programmed for this magic.

We come from the stars. All the elements that make up our planet and every atom of our bodies, the building blocks of life, come from space—specifically, from exploding stars called supernovas. So, when we think of metals and stones as being "earthy" they are really cosmic—from the universe itself. Our planet is made up of debris from space, and so are we. I hope you continue to explore this universal connection and that the practice of crystal magic expands your enjoyment of the endless mysteries of life.

Appendix

Stones and Metals: Metaphysical Correspondences

Some sources list stones as having receptive or projective energy. I believe this depends on the type of magic you're performing. Therefore, those correspondences are not given here. However, this information can be inferred based on the element associated with each. If a planetary or elemental association is not given, it is because there is no particular primary correspondence. This list has been compiled by cross-referencing dozens of sources, supplemented with my own experience working with the stones. An explanation of crystal systems follows this list.

Agate: general properties: grounding; protection; strength; promotes general good health and longevity; attunement with the earth; calming; personal development. Blue Lace: spiritual awareness, healing, inner peace. Moss: promotes agreeability, connection with plant kingdom. Trigonal.

Amazonite: balances emotions; "stone of hope," harmony and universal love; eliminates aggravation; helps perfect personal expression. Triclinic. Earth element. Uranus.

Amber (resin): positive energy; healing; sun; sensual; makes wearer irresistible. Amorphous. Sun. Fire and Earth elements.

Amethyst: promotes sobriety, helps break addictions; curbs passion; encourages spiritual awakening and peace; aids sleep, transformation, and meditation; calms, balances, and clears aura; increases psychic ability. Trigonal. Jupiter and Neptune. Water element.

Apache tear (obsidian): promotes a forgiving attitude; comfort; aids in grief acceptance; removes self-limiting barriers. Amorphous. Saturn. Fire element.

Apatite: helps manifest insights, especially past life; enhances other stones; related to service professions and humanitarian pursuits; balances; heals; stimulates clairvoyance and assists with deeper meditative states, insight, clarity and peace; awakens higher self; enhances creativity. Hexagonal.

Apophyllite: aids astral travel; gazing; reflective; encourages spiritual connections; helps one find truth. Tetragonal.

Aquamarine: "stone of courage" and tolerance; protects fishermen; spiritual awareness; psychic abilities; enhances creativity. Hexagonal. Moon. Water element.

Aragonite: centering; meditation; helps relieve stress and anger; fosters patience, reliability and practicality; helps one accept responsibilities. Orthorhombic.

Aventurine: increases prosperity, "gambler's talisman"; balances male/female energies; general healing stone (especially for pain); increases opportunity and motivation; independence—"new horizons," luck; creativity/individuality; stress-relief. Trigonal. Mercury. Air element.

Azurite: awakens psychic ability and third-eye; eliminates indecision and worry; enhances self-confidence; dissolves blockages; promotes relaxation and awareness—good for use during meditation; enhances creativity and communication with spirit guides; helps verbalize psychic experiences. Monoclinic. Venus. Water element.

Barite (desert rose): encourages one to pursue dreams—"all things are possible," encourages independence in relationships; aids detox/recovery from addictions. Orthorhombic.

Bloodstone: (also called heliotrope; a green variety of chalcedony with red hematite [iron oxide] or jasper spots) purification; promotes courage, grounding, and a "be here now" attitude; balances body; improves talents; enhances decision making. Trigonal. Mars. Fire element.

Bornite (peacock ore): freshens and renews; stimulates spirit; relieves stress and grief; a "stone of happiness"; protection from negative energy; removes barriers to goals; healing. Orthorhombic.

Brass: (a mixture of copper and zinc) healing; prosperity; protection. Sun. Fire element.

Bronzite: (magnesium and iron) "stone of courtesy" and focused action; attainment and assistance. Promotes peace; helps relieve stress and heal emotional trauma. Orthorhombic. Venus. Earth element.

Calcite: energy amplifier; aids memory; excellent for studying arts and sciences; healing (*see also* Onyx). Trigonal. (Iceland Spar is a popular formation.)

Carnelian: sexuality; personal power; physical energy; stimulates analytical capabilities and precision, concentration; compassion; present moment awareness; focus, motivation, stimulation. Trigonal. Sun. Fire element.

Celestite: revitalizing; excellent healing stone; aids pursuit of delicate arts, mental activities and problem solving; "a stone of balance"; aids astral travel and dream recall; brings calmness and harmony; eases worry; promotes communication and spiritual wisdom; clears chakras; helps distinguish between need/want. Orthorhombic. Venus, Neptune. Water element.

Chiastolite: ("cross-stone") assists with change, death and rebirth, transitions, astral travel, problem solving, creativity, practicality, and maintenance of spirituality during illness.

Chrysocolla: (a copper mineral) helps one attune to the Earth; eliminates fear; increases understanding and capacity to love; purifies home environment; aids communication; a "feminine" stone. Amorphous. Venus. Water element.

Citrine: (a variety of quartz ranging in color from pale yellow to brown) a stone of optimism and abundance; never needs cleansing—does not hold negative energy but dissipates and transmutes it; often called "the merchant's stone," use for success in education and business; aids mental clarity; teaches prosperity; good for community; dispels fear; opens communication/positive influence. Trigonal. Sun. Fire element.

Copper: energy conductor; promotes self-esteem; aid for exhaustion and sexual imbalance. Cubic. Venus. Water element.

Creedite: provides clarity of expression in the spiritual realm; helps to remove obstacles toward goal. Meditation. Monoclinic.

Cymophane (cat's eye): a variety of chrysoberyl that displays chatoyant properties (needle-like inclusions that create the "eye" effect). The gemstone careity of chrysoberyl is called alexandrite. Stimulates the intellect and awareness; stabilizing; protective. Strengthens one's approach to problems, and helps one see a situation clearly before taking action. Promotes unconditional love. Orthorhombic.

Diamond: promotes courage, purity and innocence; inspires creativity and imagination; abundance. Cubic. Sun. Fire element.

Dolomite: relieves sorrow; helps one understand that "everything happens for a reason"; removes blockages; encourages charity. Trigonal.

Emerald: "stone of successful love," associated with Venus, also encourages prosperity, legal matters, and success in business; enhances memory. Hexagonal. Venus. Earth element.

Fluorite: general properties: promotes order and reason, concentration, and meditation; "stone of discernment and aptitude"; stabilizing; helps one reach height of mental achievement—"the genius stone." Blue: calming energy; orderly communication; Clear: use for crown chrakra; aligns/cleanses aura; Green: clears negativity from a room—tidying, "minty fresh"; Purple: opens third eye; increases psychic/spiritual growth and intuition; Yellow: enhances creativity and intellectual pursuits. Cubic.

Fossil: promotes quality and excellence in one's environment.

Fuchsite: (green variety of muscovite/mica group) helps one bounce back; balancing; use for meditation for insight on practical matters; assists one in adapting to a situation. Monoclinic. Air element.

Galena: grounding and centering; "stone of harmony." Cubic. Earth element.

Garnet: "stone of health"; commitment; self-confidence; sexuality; vigor; patience; protects against thieves; sleep to remember dreams; Grossular variety: strengthens stability in lawsuits and legal matters/challenges; enhances service, fertility. Cubic. Mars. Fire element.

Geode: Earth Mother, womb; helps one see total picture. Water element.

Gold: purifies and energizes physical body, solar/male energy. Cubic. Sun. Fire element.

Granite: primarily quartz and orthoclase feldspar. Enables one to "see the big picture" and aids balance in relationships. Prosperity.

Gypsum: (selenite) lucky; ends stagnation; strengthens progress, fertility. Types include alabaster, satin spar, and selenite "rose" (crystallized): promotes awareness of self and surroundings. Monoclinic.

Hematite: purifies and balances; a "stone of the mind"; promotes self-control; grounding; psychic awareness; transforms negativity; carry to relieve stress; aids manual dexterity; helps one achieve goals. Trigonal. Saturn. Fire element.

Hemimorphite: helps one "know thyself"; decreases self-centeredness with growth toward self-respect and reaching highest potential; promotes creativity; relieves hostility. Orthorhombic.

Herkimer Diamond: (exceptionally clear quartz crystals, named for locality where first discovered, Herkimer County, NY) harmony and attunement; helps one to "be" and know you already are what you seek to become; aids relaxation and expansion of life energy; stimulates clairvoyant abilities; helps retain information/remember dreams; healing; cleansing. Trigonal.

Howlite: calms communication; helps one take action toward goals; encourages subtlety and tact; improves character; eliminates pain, stress, and rage. Monoclinic.

Iolite: (blue shades/gem quality cordierite) a third-eye stone, use for spiritual growth; stimulates shamanic visions; balances, awakens inner knowledge; can aid one in eliminating debts and accepting responsibilities; good for attaining a healthy constitution; brings harmony to self and relationships; strengthens aura. Orthorhombic.

Iron: protection, strength, grounding, healing. Cubic. Mars. Fire element.

Jade: (nephrite and jadeite, metamorphic rocks) a "dream stone"; also called the "gardener's stone"; increases vitality, harmony, inspiration, perspective, and wisdom; longevity; protective; good fortune. Venus. Water element.

Jasper: general qualities: "supreme nurturer"; healing; beauty; courage; good fortune and financial success; creativity; harmony; "an Earth Stone"; stabilizing and reduces insecurity; good for grounding after ritual. Trigonal.

Jet: (a form of fossilized wood, similar to coal) protection—dispels fearful thoughts and protects one during the pursuit of business and enhances financial stability. Amorphous. Saturn. Earth element.

Kyanite: never needs cleansing; promotes "attunement" and aligns charkas immediately; tranquility; psychic awareness and clarity; enhances creative expression; dispels anger and frustration. Triclinic.

Labradorite: protects and balances aura; aids in understanding one's destiny; enhances patience, perseverance, and inner knowing; reduces anxiety and stress; discernment in direction—"know right time"; wisdom. Triclinic. Moon. Water element.

Lapis lazuli: (lapis is actually a rock consisting mostly of the mineral lazurite, commonly containing pyrite and calcite, among other minerals) a "stone of total awareness"; amplifies spiritual and psychic awareness; promotes good judgment in practical world— wisdom; cheerful; stimulates creativity, mental clarity, and speech; sincerity; self-acceptance; boosts immune system. Cubic. Venus. Water element.

Lepidolite: reduces stress; "stone of transition" and self-love; calms environment; soothes emotions; dispels anger; a dream stone— protects against nightmares; gently induces change to "get to heart of the problem." Monoclinic. Jupiter, Neptune. Water element.

Lodestone (magnetite): balances and enhances receptivity to male/female energies; encourages one to "hold fast" to purpose; motivation; guidance. Cubic. Venus. Water element.

Malachite: transformation; clears path to goal; protection (esp. aviation); business prosperity; soothing; calming; anti-depressant; amplifies mood. Monoclinic. Venus. Earth element.

Marcasite: (a polymorph of pyrite—same chemicals, different symmetry; marcasite sold in the jewelry industry is actually pyrite) promotes insight and stimulates the intellect; promotes spiritual development; guards against impatience. Orthorhombic.

Mica: self-reflection; aids sleep. Monoclinic. Mercury. Air element.

Moonstone: feminine; lunar energy; "the traveler's stone"; helps with cycles/changes; new beginnings; intuition; insight; healing for women; heightens psychic sensitivity; calming; balancing; introspective and reflective; allows one to distinguish between needs and desires. Monoclinic. Moon. Water element.

Obsidian: protective (esp. from psychic vamps); grounding; scrying; absorbs negativity; goddess mysteries; detachment but with wisdom and love. Snowflake Obsidian: sharpens external and internal vision; reveals contrasts of life to realize unnecessary patterns; serenity in isolation and meditation; "stone of purity"; (*see also* Apache Tear). Amorphous. Saturn. Fire element.

Onyx: centering; banishes grief; enhances decision-making; relieves stress; balances male/female energy; aids detachment and self-control; heightens instinct. Trigonal. Mars. Saturn. Fire element.

Opal: releases inhibitions; awakens mystic qualities; beauty; heals spirit; contains all colors, represents all elements; aids visions and psychic journeying; affirms purpose; can be used to grant wishes and aid magical practice; allows one to fade into background when desired ("invisibility"). Amorphous.

Peacock ore: *See* Bornite.

Pearl: faith and spiritual guidance; purity; charity; innocence; sincerity. Amorphous. Moon. Water element.

Peridot: (gem quality variety of olivine—olivine can be used instead) warm; friendly; furthers understanding of change; heart and solar plexus charkas; acceptance regarding relationships; recover lost items; healing; visionary stone; frees one from envy; regulates cycles. Orthorhombic. Venus. Earth element.

Petrified wood: "change what you can and don't worry about the rest"; strength; grounding; past life meditations; support in times of crisis; transformation; prevents work stress.

Pewter: (a mixture of tin and copper, and some other metals) divination, luck, prosperity. Jupiter. Air element.

Platinum: balancing, centering; emotionally cleansing; enhances intuition. Cubic. Neptune. Water element.

Pyrite: shields from negative energy; protective; encourages health; enhances memory and understanding; practicality; strengthens will and positive outlook. Cubic. Mars. Fire element.

Quartz: Clear quartz is often called the "Master Crystal"; corresponds to all elements and astrological signs; promotes balance, purity, meditation, amplifies energy and thoughts; promotes clarity; harmony; a "stone of power"; aids communication on all levels; a magnifier, all around healer and amplifier; aids focus and transmission of energy. Trigonal. Rose: Promotes self-love, clarity of emotions, teaches forgiveness, love of others, universal love, compassion; beautifies skin; fertility; sex; cools temper. Smoky: transforms negativity; removes emotional blocks and mental barriers; adds clarity to meditation; balances; grounds; "stone of cooperation;" enhances personal pride and joy in life; enables one to let go; increases love of physical body; activates base charkas. Milky: stimulates hopes; stabilizes dreams; helps one to know self; clarity of mind; love of truth. (*See also* Citrine and Amethyst.) Rutilated: insight; "clears the way;" astral travel; helps to get to root of problem; stimulates brain function; facilitates inspiration; communication with higher self; more intense than clear quartz. Tourmalinated: creates a "solving" atmosphere; protective; polarity of energy; natural balance.

Rhodochrosite: a "stone of love and balance" aids meditation; earth healing; removes tendency toward denial and avoidance; promotes health; aids acceptance and interpretation; can bring new love into one's life; emotional balance; unites conscious and subconscious. Trigonal. Mars. Fire element.

Rhondonite: a "stone of love," balances yin-yang energy, attunement with the spirituality of the universe; helps one to achieve greatest potential; activates and energizes the heart chakra while grounding; fosters unconditional love; dispels anxiety, promotes coherence during chaotic encounters; provides calm assurance. Triclinic. Mars. Fire element.

Rhyolite: (a volcanic rock made up of mainly quartz with other minerals, feldspar is commonly included. Color combinations are usually a mixture of white, gray, green, red, and brown; sometimes it resembles granite.) "Stone of resolution"; use for change, variety and progress; meditation.

Ruby: (red corundum) "stone of nobility"; fosters prosperity and financial stability. Trigonal. Fire element.

Rutile: works to eliminate circumstances of interference. Tetragonal.

Sapphire (blue corundum): brings peace and joy; a "stone of prosperity." Black variety: centering and protection; employment opportunities; Star Sapphire (contains rutile): centering; wisdom; good fortune. Trigonal. Moon. Water element.

Serpentine: (a group of rocks that display a greenish, scale-like appearance, usually containing magnesium and iron) enhances meditative state; clears charkas; assists disorders in body and emotion with conscious direction to problem. Saturn. Fire element.

Silver: enhances mental function; soothes anger; aids circulation; relieves stress; emotional balance; improves speech; excellent energy conductor; associated with moon; female energies; receptive. Cubic. Moon. Water element.

Sodalite: logic, clarity; encourages objectivity; aids sleep; eliminates confusion; promotes fellowship; self-esteem; trust; helps one to verbalize true feelings; clears mind; helps to reach logical conclusions; helps you "lighten up." Cubic. Venus. Water element.

Sulfur: promotes an abundance of energy, flashes of inspiration, and stimulates the application of devotion toward realization of the perfection of the self; helps to gently "melt" barriers blocking progress. Orthorhombic. Sun. Fire element.

Tiger Eye: (a variety of quartz) focus and concentration; perception, understanding; grounding; wealth and money talisman; protection; psychic sight and insight; courage and strength; optimism—helps one to see things in the best light; slight masculine energy; balances; enhances creativity, integrity, and personal power; helps one manifest ideas into reality. Blue: this variety is often referred to as Falcon's Eye; promotes peace and healing; Red: protection (red is usually heat-treated for color). Trigonal. Sun. Fire element.

Tin: promotes new beginnings; divination; good fortune; prosperity. Tetragonal. Jupiter. Air element.

Topaz: (general qualities) helps to conquer fears; a "stone of true love and success in all endeavors"; promotes individuality and creativity; helps one trust decisions and see "big picture"; wealth and health; trust; strength; protection; increases abstract thought. Orthorhombic. Sun. Fire element.

Tourmaline: Black: protects against negative energy—energy deflector; enhances physical vitality; practicality; creativity; grounding; reflects negative spells. Watermelon: super activator of heart charka; allows for experience of beauty of nature; treats nervousness and emotional disorders; enhances cooperative efforts; balance; helps one to recover from heartache. Trigonal.

Turquoise: encourages spiritual attunement; use as a guide during vision quests (protection); grounding; wisdom; kindness; promotes clarity in communication; eases anxiety; aids self-awareness; helps one find "true purpose." Triclinic. Venus, Neptune. Earth element.

Unakite: heart charka and healing; emotional balance; more grounding than rose quartz; awakens love within. Monoclinic.

Vanadinite: facilitates mental processes; bridges thought and intelligence; can provide for a deep meditative state; promotes order and thrift in spending. Hexagonal.

Wulfenite: facilitates magical practice; allows for one to continue despite potential roadblocks or limitations; provides transition to psychic and astral planes. Tetragonal.

Zebra Rock (quartz and basalt): stamina; endurance (especially for athletes); gives strength in difficult times; dismisses anger; brings compassion and understanding; "look beneath the surface"; activate during full or new moon cycle.

Zircon: (not to be confused with cubic zirconia, which is synthetic) "stone of virtue"; a spiritual stone, innocence and purity; can help align chakras. Tetragonal.

Crystal Systems

There are seven basic crystal systems and these can be further divided into thirty-two classes based on various combinations of this structure. For our purposes, we'll only consider the seven basic systems. *Crystal habit* is the term used to describe the crystal's outward appearance. Think of it this way—system or structure in internal, a habit is external—like a habit a person exhibits.

These seven systems of crystal structure are important because in magic, numerology and shapes carry meaning. For example, the cube is often used as a symbol for the Earth element and a pyramid is used to represent Fire. Crystals with this particular type of structure can be used for magic related to these elements.

Remember, these systems describe the internal structure that may or may not be apparent in the actual shape of the crystal. In addition, these specific shapes offer particular characteristics we can incorporate into crystal magic.

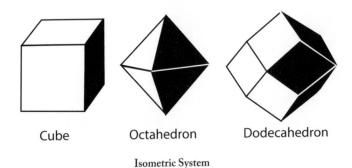

Cube   Octahedron   Dodecahedron

Isometric System

Cubic (also called isometric)—Basically, this is a cube; a three-dimensional square. Six square faces at 90 degree angles to each other. This form is also called hexahedron (fancy way of saying six sides). This structure can actually have fifteen different forms—more than any of the other crystal systems. This structure has the highest degree of crystalline symmetry. This group includes diamond, halite (rock salt), sodalite, garnet, fluorite, gold, silver, copper, platinum, and pyrite. Lapis lazuli also has this structure, but this mineral rarely crystallizes (lapis is more accurately classified as a rock). Sometimes these minerals really do form cube shapes—think of pieces of pyrite or fluorite you've seen. The ultimate form of stability and firm foundation, this form, no matter what stone it is, can provide a grounding effect or be used in spells and grids for practical purposes, reality, and structure.

....

Note: An octahedron is a shape that falls into this category. I mention this because fluorite octahedron crystals are common among collectors. Here's the confusing part—even though you may have an eight-sided fluorite octahedron, it has a cubic atomic structure inside. The symmetry of the atoms determines what kind of shape the crystal will take, but this arrangement has many possibilities.

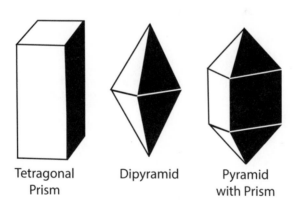

Tetragonal   Dipyramid   Pyramid
Prism   with Prism

Tetragonal System

Tetragonal—Imagine a cube being stretched at top and bottom.
....

> This is a system of three axes that meet at right angles; two
> are of equal length and the third is either longer or shorter.
> This system is based on a rectangular structure and includes
> shapes such as four-sided prisms and pyramids, eight-sided
> and double pyramids. Crystals that display this structure are
> zircon, apophyllite, wulfenite, and rutile. The characteristics of
> this form can help with balancing or uniting opposing forces.

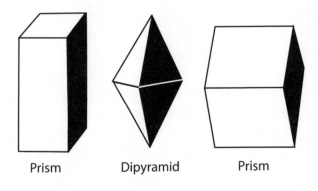

Prism   Dipyramid   Prism

Orthorhombic System

Orthorhombic—The orthorhombic system of crystals is similar to the
tetragonal system in that there are three axes that are perpendicular
to each other; however, the three axes are all unequal in length.
These axes of different lengths meet at right angles and are based
on a diamond-shaped inner structure. Shapes include rhombic
prism and pyramid. Crystals in this group include barite, sulfur,
topaz, celestite, iolite, hemimorphite, aragonite, and peridot. This
form helps with focus and perspective in a situation.

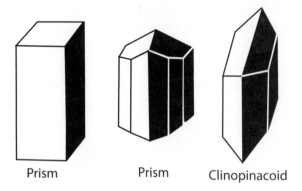

Prism   Prism   Clinopinacoid

Monoclinic System

Monoclinic—This system has three axes of different lengths. Two are at right angles and the third is inclined. This structure is based on the parallelogram. Crystals in this group are azurite, malachite, howlite, moonstone, serpentine, chrysocolla, gypsum, mica (muscovite), lazulite, staurolite, gypsum, talc, jadite, selenite, lepdiolite, and kunzite. This form is stabilizing, encouraging, and often used to obtain clarity.

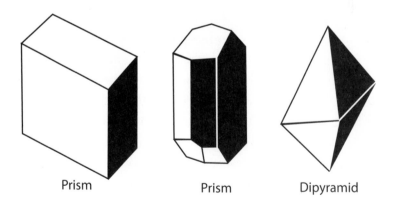

Prism   Prism   Dipyramid

Triclinic System

Triclinic—This system contains three axes of different lengths that form a pair of faces parallel to the axes and is based on a structure of three inclined angles. Crystals in this group include turquoise, amazonite, labradorite, rhodonite, and kyanite. This is the least symmetric of the group, often producing tabular style crystals. This form can assist with balance in one's personal life, perceptions, and attitudes.

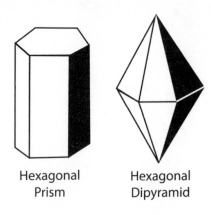

Hexagonal
Prism

Hexagonal
Dipyramid

Hexagonal System

Hexagonal—A system of four axes, one of which is shorter than the other three. These three are the same length and meet at right angles of 60 degrees. This arrangement is based on a six-sided internal structure and has seven planes of symmetry, seven axes, and a center. Some common crystal shapes are six-sided points, plus four-sided pyramids and prisms, twelve-sided pyramids, and double pyramids. Many varieties of crystals can be produced by this structure. Examples of hexagonal minerals are: emerald, aquamarine, apatite, and vanadinite. This form aids with vitality, growth, and intuition.

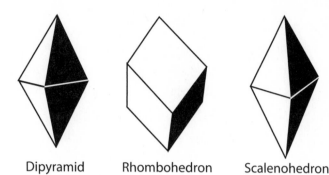

Dipyramid Rhombohedron Scalenohedron

Trigonal System

Trigonal—This system is similar to the hexagonal and is often listed as a subset of hexagonal. This system is based on a triangular structure and shapes include three-sided prisms and pyramids and rhombohedra. Crystals in this group include all varieties of quartz, sapphire, agate, calcite, carnelian, dolomite, hematite, ruby, tourmaline, onyx, bloodstone, and rhodochrosite. This form helps stimulate a balancing type of energy and is similar to hexagonal, but with a more powerful force. Trigonal has two lattice systems—hexagonal and rhombohedral.

....

Speaking of symmetry, only a sphere has perfect symmetry, and this form is not naturally found in crystals. If we want one, we have to carve a stone into that shape.

Amorphous materials lack symmetrical atomic structure (some of these are organic substances rather than minerals). They include amber, chrysocolla, jet, obsidian, opal, and pearl.

Platonic Solids

Plato's studies about the universe were not based on an actual study of science, but he proposed the idea that the qualities of things in the physical world reflected pure and perfect ideas. This is how he came to his philosophy of these five "perfect" geometric shapes. He claimed these shapes made up the entire structure of the world—the elements and the universe. Of course, we now understand this is not scientifically true, but Plato's idea of these shapes did, in fact, touch upon crystal structure. In fact, these forms were not actually discovered by Plato—they were actually known thousands of years prior to his "discovery"—stone models of these shapes have been found in the British Isles and appear to be almost four thousand years old!

These shapes are unique because they have certain characteristics: they have the same shape on each side, every line is the same length, every internal angle is the same, and each fits perfectly within a sphere. They also have duality.

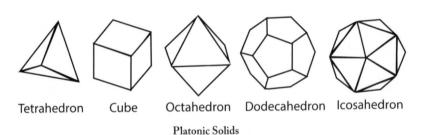

Tetrahedron   Cube   Octahedron   Dodecahedron   Icosahedron

Platonic Solids

They are regular polyhedra (many faces) or many "seats" and they are the five regular, convex, three-dimensional solids. **In crystal structure, only three of the five Platonic Solids occur naturally—the tetrahedron, cube, and octahedron** (Remember, this is internal structure, not necessarily the outward appearance of the stone. However, some stones do display this outward shape.) When working with the metaphysical properties of stones, it's useful to consider these crystalline forms.

Here are the characteristics attributed to each of the Platonic Solids:

- **Tetrahedron (a pyramid):** four equal triangular faces— Fire/Plasma (trigonal)

  » **all faces are triangular:** the base does not have a square bottom.

  » **apophyllite (often forms natural pyramids):** sometimes zircon

- **Cube:** six square faces—Earth/Solid (cubic)

  » **table salt forms (sodium chloride/halite) natural cubes:** pyrite is another good example.

- **Octahedron (dual square-bottomed pyramids):** eight equal triangular faces—Air/Gas (tetragonal)

  » **Fluorite is often found in this shape:** diamond, too. But remember, these minerals have an internal structure that is cubic—the habit (outward appearance) is sometimes octahedral.

- **Dodecahedron:** twelve pentagonal faces—(Universe/ Vacuum) a very mystical shape—twelve pentagons (twelve perfect five-sided shapes)

- **Icosahedron:** twenty equal triangular faces—Water/Liquid

Don't confuse tetrahedron with tetragronal. *Tetra* comes from Greek and means "four" but these are different things: a tetrahedron has four triangular faces; the tetragonal crystal system has two internal lattice systems—one is a stretched cube and the other is a prism. The word "tetra" is used because there are four points on the lattice. Think of a square shape (not cube) which has four points. Repeating points on an invisible lattice create the symmetry.

Correspondences for Days of the Week: Stones, Incense, and Oils

Sunday: Sun/Success, Healing, Protection, Energy
....
Stones: amber, carnelian, citrine, diamond, gold, sulfur, tiger eye, topaz
Incense/Oils: benzoin, cinnamon, copal, frankincense, rosemary

Monday: Moon/Spirituality, Intuition, Emotions, Dreams, Peace, Meditation
....
Stones: aquamarine, labradorite, moonstone, pearl, sapphire, selenite (gypsum), silver
Incense/Oils: eucalyptus, jasmine, lemon, myrrh, sandalwood

Tuesday: Mars/Protection, Strength, Courage, Sexual Energy, Healing
....
Stones: bloodstone, garnet, iron, pyrite, rhodochrosite, rhodonite
Incense/Oils: dragon's blood, pine

Wednesday: Mercury/Communication, Travel, Study
....
Stones: aventurine, mica
Incense/Oils: lavender, lemongrass, peppermint

Thursday: Jupiter/Posperity, Expansion
....
Stones: amethyst, lepidolite
Incense/Oils: star anise

Friday: Venus/Love, Abundance, Nurturing, Beauty, Happiness, Friendship
....
Stones: azurite, chrysocolla, celestite, copper, emerald, jade, lapis lazuli, lodestone, malachite, peridot, sodalite, turquoise
Incense/Oils: rose, spearmint, spikenard, vanilla

Saturday: Saturn/Longevity, Grounding, Wisdom, Purification
....
Stones: Apache tear, hematite, jet, obisidan, onyx, serpentine
Incense/Oils: patchouli

Planetary Associations

Sun: amber, brass, carnelian, citrine, diamond, gold, sulfur, tiger eye, topaz, zircon

Moon: aquamarine, celestite, labradorite, moonstone, pearl, sapphire, selenite, silver

Mercury: agate, aventurine, citrine, mica

Venus: azurite, chrysocolla, chrysoprase, calcite (blue, pink, green), copper, emerald, jade, lapis lazuli, lodestone, malachite, olivine (peridot), sodalite, tourmaline (blue, green, pink, and watermelon), turquoise

Mars: bloodstone, flint, garnet, iron, pyrite, red jasper, rhodochrosite, rhodonite, ruby

Jupiter: amethyst, lepidolite, pewter, tin

Saturn: Apache tear, galena, hematite, jet, obsidian, onyx, salt, serpentine, tourmaline (black)

Uranus: amazonite

Neptune: amethyst, lepidolite, platinum, turquoise

Chakra Stones

Root Chakra

Color: Red

Stones: agate, bloodstone, garnet, hematite, onyx, red jasper, rhodonite, ruby, tiger eye, tourmaline (black)

....

Stimulates life force; energy, vitality. Work with this chakra if you need assistance with addiction, diminished sexuality, digestive disorders. This area fosters a connection with nature. Linked to reproductive glands. Grounding. Earth element. Resting place of the life force. Associated with the sense of smell.

Sacral Chakra

Color: Orange

Stones: carnelian, citrine, jasper, moonstone, tiger eye

....

Governs the body's liquid elements—work with this chakra if you have problems with sex, nourishment, circulation, or balance. Linked to adrenaline—fight or flight (stress). Creativity, sexuality, authority, and power. Water element. Associated with the sense of taste.

Solar Plexus Chakra

Color: Yellow

Stones: aventurine quartz, citrine, malachite, rose quartz,
tiger eye, topaz
....

Treat discontent, restlessness and discouragement; fosters
inner peace. Fire element. Pancreas, liver, stomach—
individuality, personal power, link between mind and
emotion. Digestive system and autonomic nervous system.
Associated with sense of sight.

Heart Chakra

Color: Green (sometimes pink)

Stones: aventurine, emerald, green tourmaline, jade, moss agate, olivine,
rhodochrosite, rhodonite, rose quartz, watermelon tourmaline
....

Empathy, joy, friendship, heart, compassion, circulation,
thymus gland, immune system. Air element. "Higher"
emotions: tenderness, compassion, unconditional love,
universal truth. Rules the heart, lungs, upper chest, back
and bronchial tubes. Associated with sense of touch.

Throat Chakra

Color: Blue

Stones: aquamarine, blue topaz, celestite, chrysocolla, lapis lazuli,
moonstone, opal, pearl, turquoise
....

Helps one open to new experiences and self-expression;
governs the thyroid, hunger, thirst, eyes, ears, nose, throat,
lungs, voice, and speech. Ether element. Communication—
writing, speech, and art. Associated with the sense of hearing.

Third Eye/Brow Chakra

Color: Indigo

Stones: amethyst, clear quartz, fluorite, lapis lazuli, sapphire, sodalite
....

> Understanding and insight, intuition, self-knowledge,
> perception; eyes, nose, face, senses; mysticism; telepathic
> energy. Associated with the sixth sense—insight and wisdom.

Crown Chakra

Color: Violet

Stones: amethyst, celestite, clear quartz, diamond, gold, violet fluorite
....

> Inner development, spirituality, enlightenment; seat of the
> soul—perfection of body, mind, and spirit—cosmic energy.
> Transmutation.

Elemental Associations

Earth: agate, amazonite, amber, bronzite, emerald, fossils of plants
and land animals, galena, granite, green jasper, jet, malachite, olivine
(peridot), petrified wood, salt, tourmaline (green and black), turquoise

Air: aventurine, fluorite, fuchsite, mica, pewter, pumice, tin

Fire: amber, bloodstone, brass, carnelian, citrine, diamond, garnet,
gold, hematite, iron, obsidian (Apache tear), onyx, rhodochrosite,
rhodonite, ruby, sulfur, tiger eye, topaz, zircon

Water: amethyst, aquamarine, azurite, blue lace agate, blue tourmaline,
celestite, chryscolla, copper, fossils of sea animals and shells, geodes,
jade, labradorite, lapis lazuli, lepidolite, lodestone, moonstone, pearl,
platinum, sapphire, silver, sodalite

Seasonal Associations

Spring: amethyst, emerald, peridot, pink topaz

Summer: fire opal, garnet, ruby

Autumn: sapphire, topaz, tourmaline

Winter: clear quartz, diamond, labradorite, moonstone, pearl, turquoise

Stones by Use

Here is a listing of groups of stones commonly used for a purpose. Keep in mind that each stone has subtle differences—I have noted some of the more important distinctions here. Start here for quick reference by topic, then examine the properties of each stone to fine-tune your choice.

Attraction/Lust: amber, carnelian

Balancing: apatite, aventurine, bloodstone, bornite, celestite, clear quartz, dolomite, hematite, labradorite (aura), lodestone, moonstone, onyx, platinum, rhodochrosite, silver, smoky quartz, tiger eye, tourmalinated quartz, turquoise, unakite, watermelon tourmaline

Cleaning/Purification: blue fluorite (aura), chrysocolla (home), citrine, clear quartz, gold, green fluorite, Herkimer diamond, kyanite

Creativity: apatite, aquamarine, aventurine, azurite, blue topaz, celestite, diamond, jade (nephrite), kyanite, lapis lazuli, sodalite, stillbite, tiger eye, turquoise, yellow fluorite

Communication: creedite (in spirit realm), howlite, sodalite

Dispel negativity, dissolve blockages, increase positive energy and happiness: amber, apatite, black tourmaline, bornite ("stone of happiness"), calcite, celestite, clear quartz, copper (conductor), dolomite, green fluorite, gypsum, hematite, malachite, obsidian, peridot, pyrite, silver (conductor), smoky quartz, sulfur, tiger eye, topaz, turquoise, zebra rock

Fertility: grossular garnet, gypsum, rose quartz

Good fortune: aventurine, gypsum, jasper, pewter, topaz

Grounding, centering, focus: agate, black tourmaline, bloodstone ("be here now"), carnelian, fluorite, galena, hematite, iron, jasper, lodestone (direction/guidance), obsidian, smoky quartz, tiger eye

Healing (general): amber, bloodstone (blood), bronzite (emotional) calcite, celestite, clear quartz, gold, Herkimer diamond, iron, jasper (supreme nurturer), moonstone (women), peridot, unakite

Health/Longevity: agate, brass, garnet, jade, lapis lazuli (immune system), pyrite, rhodochrosite, tiger eye, topaz

Love, harmony, peace, beauty, hope: clear quartz, emerald, galena, Herkimer diamond, jasper (beauty), opal, peridot, rhodochrosite, rhodonite, rose quartz (universal/gentle love), stillbite, unakite (more grounding than rose quartz), watermelon tourmaline
....

Note: Rhodochrosite (manganese ore) and rhodonite are often confused with one another. Both can be used for love—both are ruled by Mars and the element of Fire, so they're stronger in love spells than rose quartz—more passion-oriented. Both are used for balanced love. Rhodonite is more directed at self-love and unconditional love; rhodochrosite brings new love into one's life, can help facilitate earth healing and aids acceptance—an excellent stone for balancing. The *rhodo-* in both names refers to the rose color. Rhodochrosite is generally prettier, often streaked with white calcite, and can form crystals. Rhodonite is more grounding and harder, often associated with pyrite or display veins of black manganese; crystals are rare.

Meditation: amethyst, azurite, clear quartz, fluorite, petrified wood (past lives), rhodochrosite, serpentine, smoky quartz, snowflake obsidian, vanadinate

Mental acuity, intellect, wisdom: apatite, aquamarine, bloodstone (decisions), calcite, carnelian, celestite, citrine, clear quartz, fluorite, hematite, Herkimer diamond, jade, lapis lazuli, milky quartz, pyrite (memory), rutilated quartz, silver, sodalite, tiger eye, topaz, tourmalinated quartz, vanadinite, zebra rock

Prosperity/Success: aventurine, brass, citrine, diamond, emerald, gold, malachite, pewter, rhodonite (reach potential), tiger eye

Protection: agate, black tourmaline, brass, clear quartz, garnet, iron, jade, lepidolite (nightmares), malachite (air travel), moonstone (travel), obsidian, tiger eye, turquoise

Psychic ability, awareness, insight, intuition: apatite, apophyllite, azurite, calcite, celestite, hematite, Herkimer diamond, kyanite, labradorite, lapis lazuli, moonstone, opal, pewter (divination), purple fluorite, silver, tiger eye. Third eye stimulation: amethyst, apatite, apophyllite, azurite, clear quartz, fluorite (purple), Herkimer diamond, iolite, kyanite, lapis lazuli, moonstone, opal, wulfenite

Recover lost objects: peridot

Sleep/Dreams: amethyst, celestite, garnet, jade, lepidolite (guard against nightmares), mica, milky quartz, sodalite, topaz

Spirituality: amethyst, apophyllite, aquamarine, celestite, chiastolite (during illness), clear quartz, creedite (communication in spirit realm), diamond, opal, turquoise (vison quests/journey)

Strength, courage, confidence, self-esteem: agate, aquamarine ("stone of courage"), azurite, barite rose, citrine, copper (self-esteem), garnet, iron, jasper (courage), lapis lazuli, sodalite, topaz, zebra rock (physical endurance)

Stress/Anxiety relief, ease of emotional disorders, relaxation, calming: agate, amazonite, amethyst, aventurine, azurite, blue fluorite, bornite, copper, diamond, jasper, Herkimer diamond, kyanite, labradorite, malachite, moonstone, onyx, petrified wood (work environments), platinum, rhodonite, rose quartz, silver, turquoise, unakite, watermelon tourmaline

Transitions/Transformation, comfort, self-reflection: amethyst, Apache tear, chiastolite, ledpidolite, malachite, mica, petrified wood, rhodochrosite, sulfur, tin (new beginnings)

Travel: apophyllite (astral), chiastolite (astral), moonstone, turquoise (shamanic journeying/vision quests)

Colors

This list includes the basic information about color use in magic, as well as some correspondences for numerology and a bit of folklore. The color of a stone often indicates its type of use in magic.

Red has always been associated with passion, probably because our blood is red. It has also been used to denote royalty, power, and leadership and has been used to symbolize war and vengeance. Red has been linked to the number 9 in numerology, and is associated with the god Mars. The rays of the color red are heat-giving, so it's no wonder red, a "warm" color, has these meanings assigned to it. Other traits associated with red are: physical energy, stamina, sexuality, activity, survival, and passion.

Orange is a color that can be used to dissolve blockages and barriers to a goal—it is essentially red tempered with yellow and is often an effective healing color because it contains the strength of red with the softness of the sunny shade of yellow. Characteristics of orange are: vitality, ambition, fertility, creativity, and stress reduction. It does not have a numerical association.

Yellow and gold have long been associated with the sun and the positive attributes of its life-giving rays. Other key words: optimism, success, satisfaction, generosity, organization, and order. It does not have a numerical association.

Green has often been thought to be the most pleasing color to the eye—the lush green of forests and plants symbolize fertility, and green is often considered to represent hope, happiness, and change. Associated with the number 5, and the god Mercury (and some sources say the goddess Venus as well). Green is often used to represent nature and, because this color is lovely to look at, it was believed to cure ailments pertaining to eyesight. Also characteristic of friendship, freedom, harmony, peace, empathy, renewal, and adaptation.

Blue has long been symbolic of the heavens, due to the color of the sky. It's associated with beauty, the goddess Venus, and the number 6. Blue is also associated with wisdom and spirituality, faithfulness, loyalty, responsibility, respect, understanding, and the smooth flow of communication (due to its relationship with the throat chakra); sometimes used to stimulate inspiration. A soothing, cool, and calming color.

Violet is sometimes linked to justice and judgment, also a color of royalty and industry. It's associated with age and wisdom, the god Jupiter, and the number 3. In addition, shades of purple and violet represent spirituality, insight, transformation, determination, and devotion. Think of this color, especially in its darker shades, containing the qualities of its combination of red and blue. This means purple contains the coolness of blue with the heat and energy of red.

White or colorless stones (and pearls) always seem to be linked to the moon. Sometimes, however, the diamond, due to its radiant sparkle, was associated with the sun. White also represents purity and friendship. In some cultures, white is a mourning color. White is linked to the number 7. White also represents purity, sincerity, clarity, truth, innocence, perfection, and immortality. White contains potential since it's the complete spectrum of all colors. Also often used to represent spirituality.

Black is a color of gravity and wisdom—a somber color, and also a color of mourning in some societies. It is usually associated with Saturn, and the number 8. Other characteristics are: elegance, security, detachment, and seclusion. Black and white are true opposites, yet similar in some ways: black contains all colors and absorbs them and so since black, like white, contains all colors, they have this trait in common. Yet black holds all the colors in while white sends them out. Black represents rest and repose, the inward journey, the soul—as opposed to the pure white light of spirit, an uplifting and outward expression. Black and white are most commonly seen together in the yin-yang symbol. Black also represents things hidden, a time of dormancy, and preparation for growth—it's also a good grounding and protective color.

Shapes

Square: order, stability, four directions

Circle: continuity, spirituality, connectedness, cycles

Triangle: trinity, body-mind-spirit,

Spiral: growth and movement (our DNA forms in spirals; the DNA spiral is a golden section)

Glossary

Alchemy: A practice that most likely began with the Taoists in China and the Pythagoreans in Greece after the sixth century BCE—the goal of changing substances, such as ordinary metal, into gold. Their practice of changing substances from liquids to gases and back again invented the process of distillation.

Amorphous: Literally, "without form"; applied to rocks and minerals that lack definite crystal structure.

Amulet: Magical item worn or carried for protection or to repel something (such as negativity). *See* talisman.

Archetype: As defined by Carl Jung, types of universal human instincts, impulses, characters, etc., which have become the common idea of myths.

Aromatherapy: The use of essential oils from plants to affect well-being. Scents are inhaled or used in bath or massage.

Aura: Subtle energy field that is said to surround a person or object (*See also* subtle bodies).

Charge: In magical terms, to mentally project a specific type of energy into an object.

Chatoyant: fibrous inclusions (usually of the mineral rutile) in a stone, causing an "eye" effect. This can be seen in many types of stones including chrysoberyl, beryl (aquamarine), quartz (tiger eye), tourmaline, moonstone. This natural pattern can also be artificially created in glass. Sometimes these inclusions create a star effect called asterism. The light reflection creates the pattern. Stones are typically cut into a cabochon to highlight this effect.

Cleavage: The property of a mineral that allows it to break along a smooth plane surface.

Conduction: In scientific terms, the transfer of heat by molecular motion from a region of high temperature to a region of lower temperature.

Consecration: The act of dedicating an item or place as sacred or to be used for special purpose.

Crystal: A solid material with an orderly atomic arrangement.

Crystal habit: The actual form of a crystal; determined by the shape and relative proportions of the crystal faces.

Crystal symmetry: The repeat pattern of crystal faces, caused by the ordered internal arrangement of a mineral's atoms.

Crystal system: The structure or lattice arrangement of atoms in the internal structure of a crystal.

Dominant/Projective hand: In magical practice, the hand you write with, or use most often. Used to project energy.

Element: In magic, refers to the four classical ones: Earth, Air, Fire, and Water, without which life as we know it would not be possible—Spirit is sometimes considered to be a fifth element.

Elixir: As it refers to magical gem elixirs, placing a stone in water for a length of time, infusing the water with the metaphysical crystal energy.

Essence: Like an elixir, but created for long-term storage by using a preservative of alcohol or vinegar.

Fibonacci Sequence: Pattern discovered in the twelfth century by Leonardo Fibonacci. Starting with 0 and 1, each new number in the series is the sum of the two before it. 0, 1, 1, 2, 3, 5, 8, 13, 21, 34, 55, 89, 144 ... This pattern occurs in nature in many places: the seed heads of flowers, the spiral of pine cones and pineapples, and the way stems and leaves are arranged on plants.

Fossil: The remains of a plant or animal buried in sediment. Fossils are the surviving hard parts of the organism or impression of the organism in the sediment.

Golden Ratio: Also called Golden Mean, Golden Rectangle, and Divine Proportion. A golden rectangle can always be divided into a square and another golden rectangle over and over again. The key to this special form is the ratio of height to width. This proportion is claimed to be especially pleasing to the eye, and it's found in many natural objects and can be identified in many famous works of art and architecture.

Infusion: An extract made by soaking plant material in warm or hot water.

Lead crystal: A type of glass containing a high proportion of lead within crystallized quartz, used especially for decorative items (also known as Austrian crystal).

Magma: Hot, molten material from deep underground, usually associated with volcanic eruptions. Magma that reaches the surface is called lava.

Magnetism: A magnetic field is a field of attractive or repulsive forces generated by moving or spinning electric charges. The ore magnetite is a naturally occurring mineral that contains a large amount of iron and sometimes becomes magnetized by the earth's magnetic field.

Mandala: In Buddhism and Hinduism, a diagram having spiritual and/or ritual significance. *Mandala* is the Sanskrit word for "circle."

Mantra: A sound, syllable, or words that are repeated like a chant or affirmation—intended to be used to achieve transformation, from Eastern religious practices.

Metal: Solid elements (with the exception of mercury, the only liquid metal) with high melting points; good conductors of electricity; most are shiny in appearance.

Metaphysical: The philosophical study of the ultimate causes and underlying nature of things.

Mineral: Naturally forming, usually inorganic, crystalline substances with characteristic physical and chemical properties determined by their composition and internal structure.

Neo-Pagan: "New" Paganism, referring to modern polytheistic religious beliefs, including Wicca and modern Witchcraft.

New Age: a term often used to refer to eclectic beliefs and practices that rose to popularity in the U.S. during the 1960s and 1970s and have evolved into current use—a collection of esoteric and spiritual techniques that blend Eastern and Western philosophies, ancient and modern. Often including astrology, crystal healing, transcendental meditation, aromatherapy, etc.

Ore: A metal-bearing mineral or rock, or a native metal, often mined for profit; a mineral or natural product serving as a source of some nonmetallic substance, as sulfur.

Organic: Pertaining to or derived from life, usually in reference to organisms. Chemically, an organic compound has hydrogen or nitrogen directly linked with carbon.

Piezoelectric effect: The generation of an electrical charge when pressure is applied to a nonconductive material. This is what makes quartz effective in watches.

Polymorph: The same chemical compound that crystallizes in different forms.

Projective hand (dominant): In magical practice, the hand you use to write with, or use most often. Use this hand to project energy.

Radiation: The emission and propagation of radiant energy—either atomic, by radioactive substances, or spectral, as in light.

Receptive hand: In magical practice, the hand you don't write with, or use less often. Used to receive energy.

Runes: Ancient writing system originating in Northern Europe.

Sabbat: Eight sacred times of the year that Wiccans celebrate, based on seasonal changes.

Sachet: A small bag often filled with perfumed powder or other scented material such as dried herbs and flowers.

Scrying: Process of divination that involves gazing into a crystal, water, or other medium to see images or symbols.

Shaman: Often a medicine man or woman within a tribe or clan; someone who practices spiritual and healing arts, divination, and communication with the spirit world.

Smudging: Ritual cleansing of an object or place using the smoke of burning herbs and/or resins.

Snuffer: A bell- or dome-shaped object, often at the end of a stick or wand, used to extinguish a candle flame.

Spectrum: Radiation (usually visible light) broken into its component wavelengths.

Subtle bodies: Pertaining to crystal healing and magic, the energies surrounding the body: etheric, closest to physical; emotional, feelings; mental, thoughts and mental processes; astral, personality; causal, links personality to collective unconscious; soul or celestial is the higher self; and spiritual presents access to universal energy but is still individual.

Talisman: Magical item worn, carried, or created to attract something (i.e., good fortune).

Translucent: Pertaining to a solid or liquid medium through which light will travel but no clear image is formed. Frosted glass is translucent.

Transparent: Pertaining to a sold or liquid medium through which light will travel and form a clear image. Window glass is transparent.

Yin and Yang: in Chinese philosophy, Yin is "darkness" and Yang is "light" as seen as cosmic powers that interact to create everything in the universe. Not literally dark and light, but a union of opposites that depends on each other—light and shadow, moist and dry, masculine and feminine. Yin is the feminine and Yang is the masculine.

Bibliography

Aveni, Anthony. *Behind the Crystal Ball: Magic, Science, and the Occult from Antiquity Through the New Age.* Boulder, CO: University Press of Colorado, 2002.

———. *Conversing with the Planets: How Science and Myth Invented the Cosmos.* Boulder, CO: University of Colorado Press, 2002.

Barnes-Svarney, Patricia, ed. *The New York Public Library Science Desk Reference.* New York: MacMillian, 1995.

Benner, Rev. Bette Jo. "Alchemy." www.denverspiritualcommunity.com.

Bishop, A. C., A. R. Woolley, and W. R. Hamilton. *Guide to Minerals, Rocks, and Fossils.* New York: Firefly Books, 2005.

Bruce-Mitford, Miranda. *The Illustrated Book of Signs and Symbols.* New York: Barnes and Noble Books, 2004.

Buchan, Jamie. *Easy as Pi: The Countless Ways We Use Numbers Every Day.* Pleasantville, NY: Reader's Digest Books, 2009.

Chesterman, Charles W., and Kurt E. Lowe. *National Audubon Society Field Guide to North American Rocks and Minerals.* New York: Knopf, 1979.

Cunningham, Scott. *Cunningham's Encyclopedia of Crystal, Gem, and Metal Magic.* St. Paul, MN: Llewellyn Worldwide, 1992.

Dietrich, R. V., and Brian J. Skinner. *Gems, Granites, and Gravels.* Cambridge, UK: Cambridge University Press, 1990.

Dubin, Lois Sherr. *North American Indian Jewelry and Adornment.* New York: Harry N. Abrams, 1999.

Dunne, Brenda J., and Robert G. Jahn. "Consciousness and Anomalous Physical Phenomena." Princeton Engineering Anomalies Research and School of Engineering and Applied Science, Princeton University. http://www.princeton.edu/~pear /pdfs/1995-consciousness-anomalous-physical-phenomena.pdf.

Eid, Alain. *1000 Photos of Minerals and Fossils.* New York: Barron's Educational Series, 1998.

Elsbeth, Marguerite. *Crystal Medicine.* St. Paul, MN: Llewellyn Worldwide, 2000.

Emoto, Masaru. Translated by David A. Thayne. *The Hidden Messages in Water.* Hillsboro, OR: Beyond Words Publishing, 2004.

Erickson, Jon. *An Introduction to Fossils and Minerals.* New York: Facts on File, 2000.

"Fibonacci Numbers in Nature and the Golden Ratio." World-Mysteries.com.

Gillotte, Galen. *Sacred Stones of the Goddess*. St. Paul, MN: Llewellyn Worldwide, 2003.

Goodman, Linda. *Linda Goodman's Star Signs*. New York: St. Martin's Press, 1997.

Grande, Lance, and Allison Augustyn. *Gems and Gemstones: Timeless Natural Beauty of the Mineral World*. University of Chicago Press: 2009.

Gubelin, Eduard, and Franz-Xaver Erni. *Gemstones: Symbols of Beauty and Power*. Tucson, AZ: Geoscience Press: 2000.

Guhr, Andreas, and Jorg Nagler. *Crystal Power: Mythology and History*. Baden-Baden, Germany: Earthdancer Books, 2006.

Haagensen, Erling, and Henry Lincoln. *The Templars' Secret Island*. New York: Barnes and Noble Books, 2002.

Hall, Manly P. *The Secret Teachings of All Ages*. New York: Tarcher-Penguin, 2003.

Harton, Robyn A. "Potentially Toxic or Harmful Stones." www.crystalsandjewelry.com.

Johnson, Ole. *Minerals of the World*. New Jersey: Princeton University Press, 1994.

Jones, Wendy, and Barry Jones. *The Magic of Crystals*. New York: Harper Collins, 1996.

Jung, Carl G., M. L. von Franz, Joseph L. Henderson, Jolande Jacobi, and Aniela Jaffe. *Man and His Symbols*. New York: Laurel, 1964.

Krauskopf, Konrad B., and Arthur Beiser. *The Physical Universe*. 9th edition. New York: McGraw Hill, 2000.

Kunz, George Frederick. *The Curious Lore of Precious Stones*. New York: Bell Publishing, 1989.

Lilly, Simon. *The Complete Illustrated Guide to Crystal Healing*. New York: Harper Collins, 2002.

Marriott, Susannah. *Witches, Sirens and Soothsayers*. London: Spruce, 2008.

Martineau, John, ed. *Quadrivium: The Four Classical Liberal Arts of Number, Geometry, Music, and Cosmology*. New York: Walker and Co., 2010.

Melody. *Love is in the Earth: A Kaleidoscope of Crystals*. Wheat Ridge, CO: Earth-Love Publishing, 1995.

Molyneaux, Brian Leigh. *The Sacred Earth*. London: Duncan Baird, 1995.

Parker, Julia, and Derek Parker. *Astrology*. New York: Dorling Kindersley, 2007.

Peschek-Bohmer, Flora, and Gisela Schreiber. *Healing Crystals and Gemstones*. Old Saybrook, CT: Konecky & Konecky, 2003.

Pollack, Rachel. *The Complete Illustrated Guide to Tarot*. London: HarperCollins, 2001.

The Quartz Page. http://www.quartzpage.de/gro_text.html.

Rockhounding Arkansas. 2011. http://www.rockhoundingar.com /types.php.

Roob, Alexander. *Alchemy and Mysticism*. London: Taschen, 2009.

Simpson, Liz. *The Book of Crystal Healing*. New York: Sterling Publishing, 1997.

Smigel, Barbara. "Fossilized Plant Material as Gems." www
.bwsmigel.info.

Smith, Karl J. *The Nature of Mathematics*. 8th edition. Pacific Grove,
CA: Brooks Cole, 1998.

Sofianides, Anna S., and George E. Harlow. *Gems and Crystals*. New
York: Simon and Schuster, 1990.

"Working With Crystals." Peacefulmind.com.

Index